Lernkrimi Englisch

Learning by Killing

W0085861

Michael Bacon
Alison Romer
Sarah Trenker

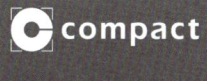

Weitere Informationen zu Compact Lernkrimis finden Sie am Ende des Buches und unter www.lernkrimi.de.

© Compact Verlag GmbH
Baierbrunner Str. 27, 81379 München
Ausgabe 2017

Redaktion: Helga Aichele, Ursula Bachhausen
Fachkorrektur: Fiona Cain, Nathalie Russell
Produktion: Ute Hausleiter
Titelillustration: Karl Knospe
Lernkrimi-Logo: Carsten Abelbeck
Gestaltung: EKH Werbeagentur GbR, textum GmbH
Umschlaggestaltung: red.sign GbR, Stuttgart; Hartmut Baier

ISBN 978-3-8174-1388-1
381741388/1

www.compactverlag.de, www.lernkrimi.de, www.facebook.com/lernkrimi

# Vorwort

Liebe Leserin, lieber Leser,

sicher zum Lernerfolg – mit Spaß und Spannung! Die Compact Lernkrimis mit ihrer Kombination aus Lektüre und didaktischem Übungsanteil eignen sich hervorragend, um breite Sprachkompetenzen in der Fremdsprache zu erwerben. Der Lernende wird dabei durch die spannende Handlung, das angemessene Sprachniveau und den stetig ansteigenden Schwierigkeitsgrad der Übungen gefördert und motiviert.

Entwickelt nach neuesten Erkenntnissen der Fremdsprachendidaktik, sind Compact Lernkrimis das ideale Medium für einen Lernerfolg im Selbststudium. Durch die kleinen Texteinheiten und den hohen Übungsanteil sind sie aber auch als Unterrichtslektüre bestens geeignet.

So lernen Sie mit Compact Lernkrimis:

- **Mit Begeisterung lernen:** Die packende Krimihandlung motiviert Sie beim Lesen des englischen Originaltextes.
- **Wissen intensivieren und erweitern:** Durch die Kombination aus didaktisch aufbereiteter Lektüre und textbezogenen Übungen testen und trainieren Sie Ihre Sprachkenntnisse effektiv. Vokabelangaben auf jeder Seite unterstützen Sie beim Lesen.
- **Systematisch lernen:** Knüpfen Sie an Ihr individuelles Sprachniveau an und setzen Sie sich eigene Lernziele.
- **Unabhängig sein:** Lernen Sie individuell – wo und wann immer Sie wollen.

Viel Spaß beim **spannenden Erlernen der englischen Sprache** wünscht Ihnen

Prof. Dr. Christiane Neveling
Didaktik der romanischen Sprachen, Universität Leipzig

Inhalt

Learning by Killing

Michael Bacon

Check-In

Tracy Dean, the secretary, smiles at the young man.

"Now, what's your name?"

He must be French, she thinks. He's wearing a raincoat in the middle of July – and he's looking at the women in the corner of the room. The young man laughs loudly and grins at Tracy.

"My name? Pierre! Pierre Leclerc, of course!"

His teeth are perfectly white, and his long, black hair **matches** his deep, brown eyes. The two women in the corner **giggle** and **stare** at Pierre Leclerc. He **shrugs** his shoulders, and they giggle again.

"Well, Pierre, your class is B1. Your teacher is Jim Ryan. Would you like a cup of coffee? Join the others over there. They're in your class, too. Next please!"

to match (with)	(zusammen) passen; vergleichen (mit)
to giggle	kichern
to stare	starren
to shrug	die Achseln zucken
plump	pummelig, mollig
to shuffle	*hier:* schlurfen
glasses *pl*	Brille; Gläser
by the way	übrigens

A short, rather **plump** man **shuffles** forward. He's wearing **glasses**.

"My name is Mr Schultze. I am a German. Do you want my passport?"

"No," says Tracy, "that isn't necessary, Mr Schultze. You're on my list – and you're in Jim Ryan's class as well. Follow Pierre and have a cup of coffee. **By the way**, we always use first names here at Church Hill. My name is Tracy – and yours?"

Mr Schultze hesitates and then almost whispers.

"It's Karl. Karl with a K!"

"Pleased to meet you, Karl. How was your journey?"

to hesitate	zögern
to whisper	flüstern
to offend	kränken, beleidigen
to tick off	abhaken

Karl Schultze takes a step backwards. He is a little uncertain about the question. The flight from Hanover to London was punctual, efficient and cheap. The Underground from Heathrow to Waterloo Station was also cheap, but with two heavy suitcases it was, quite honestly, unpleasant. The train to Eastcastle was late and slow, with too many people. The taxi from the station was fast, much too fast, and also very expensive. Can he say all this in one sentence, or does he need his dictionary? He doesn't want to offend Tracy, who is very attractive – and very friendly. Karl remembers a phrase from his English class in Gifhorn!

"Let's cut it short!" he laughs. "My journey was excellent."

Tracy ticks off Karl's name and points to the corner with the coffee. Karl, pleased with himself, walks towards the girls. He puts down his two suitcases, takes a cup of coffee and then studies his dictionary.

Tracy Dean continues to note all the new arrivals and send them to the tables with coffee and tea. In all, there are twenty students who want to stay for three weeks at The Church Hill School for English. Three weeks in Eastcastle, a little village on the South Coast. It is not very far from Brighton, about fifteen minutes by train, and the beaches and the cliffs are superb.

In England und den USA ist die Anrede mit dem Vornamen sehr viel häufiger als im Deutschen. Anders als das Duzen im Deutschen ist dies nicht unbedingt Ausdruck einer engeren persönlichen Beziehung.

Exercise 1: Match up the opposites. Welche Gegenteile gehören zusammen? Ordnen Sie zu!

1. laugh
2. plump
3. whisper
4. cheap
5. late
6. short
7. superb
8. heavy
9. fast

☐ terrible
☐ light
☐ cry
☐ slow
☐ shout
☐ expensive
☐ slim
☐ tall
☐ early

The school is a large Victorian building with a long garden at the back and a **drive** at the front. There's one car parked near the steps that lead to the front door. But what a car! A Rolls Royce from the late fifties! It **sparkles** in the afternoon sunshine. This **is the pride and joy of** Colonel

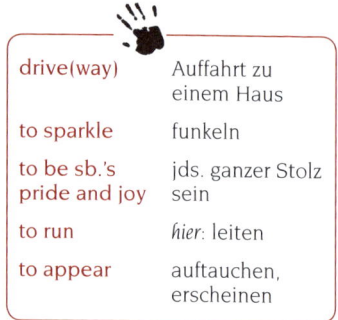

drive(way)	Auffahrt zu einem Haus
to sparkle	funkeln
to be sb.'s pride and joy	jds. ganzer Stolz sein
to run	*hier*: leiten
to appear	auftauchen, erscheinen

Lessons, the owner of Church Hill School for English. He's a retired army officer, and he **runs** his school with military precision. However, he doesn't **appear** in the building too often. Most of the time, he's at the 19th hole of Eastcastle's Golf Club. This **ex-**

pression is often confusing for foreign students. Golf? Aren't there only 18 holes? That's quite right, but people often call the club house the 19th hole or the "watering hole". This is a perfect place where you can relax and have a drink – or two, or three and often even more.

Occasionally the Colonel comes to the school to check the accounts and the reservations for the next course. When

expression	(Gesichts-)Ausdruck
confusing	verwirrend
accounts *pl*	Geschäftsbücher
mock	*hier*: gespielt; falsch
mobile	Handy
speck	Körnchen; Pünktchen
to switch on	*hier*: (Motor) an-lassen
marvellous	wunderbar, fantas-tisch
⚡ money for old rope	leicht verdientes Geld
fee	*hier*: Schulgeld; Gebühr

he leaves, he raises his hand in mock salute and always shouts: "Any problems, call me on the mobile. I'll be at Number 19." Then he marches down the steps and gets into his car. He wipes a few specks of dust off the passenger seat and, like a small boy opening a Christmas present, he switches on the engine. He listens carefully. No, he can't hear a thing, so all is in order.

A "Roller", 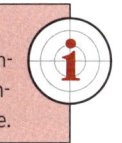 he says to himself, is a car that must be seen and not heard. What a marvellous life! All the summer courses are full. This language school business is money for old rope! The students pay the exorbitant fees before they start; the teachers get their low salary four weeks after their teaching finishes. And the difference between what comes in and what goes out lands in my bank account. In about five years, I'll be a millionaire! I can move to the South of France and forget this stupid little town for ever! And then he drives off to

Was Colonel Lessons hier liebevoll als „Roller" bezeich-net, ist natürlich - ganz stan-desgemäß - sein Rolls Royce.

the golf club and his first gin and tonic of the day.

Tracy is a very attractive woman in her mid-thirties. She's taller than Colonel Lessons and has long, blond hair and a healthy, sun-tanned complexion. This comes from her interest in sailing. When she's not at Church Hill, you can almost always find her at the harbour, working on her small yacht.

Like all sailors, male or female, she spends more time painting and cleaning her boat than actually sailing. She was born in Eastcastle and loves the relaxed atmosphere of a small,

complexion	Teint
male	männlich
coastal	Küsten…
Punch and Judy show	Kasperletheater
fairly	ziemlich
staff	Kollegium; Personal
⚡ conman	Schwindler
case	Fall

coastal town. The fishing boats, the promenade with its terraced houses and shops, the three pubs for the tourists, the seagulls screech-ing over the small pier, the Punch and Judy show next to the entrance.

Yes, she says to herself, when she's cleaning a railing or washing down the deck, this is heaven on earth! And the job is marvellous, I can't complain at all. Well, except for the boss.

Tracy doesn't really like the Colonel. She's fairly sure that he only runs the school to make a profit. He's a businessman! But there are always fresh faces. Every summer new students, as well as new teachers. Colonel Lessons has only one permanent member of staff – and this is his daughter, Rose. All the other teachers are looking for summer work; they are often people who want to earn a little extra money teaching their mother tongue – sometimes teachers who are between jobs. Occasionally a conman who has no idea how to teach the language but needs the money. For example Henry, last year. A sad case, in fact a complete and total failure. But – so it goes. Not everyone can be like Jim Ryan, the new Irish recruit for this summer. His **contract** is for two courses, six weeks in all. The second course is just begin-

| contract | Vertrag |
| ⚡ pep talk | aufmunternde Worte |

ning. This Sunday, as she begins to paint the mast, Tracy thinks about the changes in her life during the last three weeks. In fact, she's in love with Jim Ryan. OK, it is true that he is a little younger than she is – 29, in fact – but he's so romantic. This may be her last chance.

Exercise 2: Odd one out. Welches Wort ist das „schwarze Schaf"? Unterstreichen Sie das nicht in die Reihe passende Wort!

1. attractive   ugly   beautiful   handsome
2. yacht   boat   car   ship
3. building   house   school   garden
4. leave   depart   arrive   stay
5. clever   stupid   silly   ridiculous
6. sailor   secretary   soldier   officer
7. small   tiny   miniature   huge
8. pier   seagull   harbour   coastal town
9. students   teacher   sailor   pupils

Rose, Colonel Lessons's daughter, is giving a **pep talk** to the staff.

"Now, we're all here. The students are here as well. Teaching begins on Monday and, as you know, the motto of Church Hill is

11

'Learning by Doing'. Each of you has five students, and we expect a presentation, in the widest sense of the word, after the three weeks of teaching. You all have a theme. Yours, Terry, is 'English Food', are you happy with that?"

Terry **nods** and makes a few **notes**.

"I'll **manage**," he says. "We can put a menu together that covers everything. With prices and re- cipes. No problem!"

Rose continues. "Janet, your group should concentrate on music. Anything connected with music. And Patricia – or do you prefer Pat?"

Patricia Jones shrugs her shoulders. Rose smiles.

"OK – Pat! Your theme is 'The Village Fair'. You know, the standard stuff about **jumble sales**, **sack races**, and so on."

Patricia Jones feels uncomfortable. She comes from

to nod	nicken
note	Notiz, Zettel
to manage to do sth.	es schaffen, etw. zu tun
recipe	Kochrezept
jumble sale	Flohmarkt, Basar
sack race	Sackhüpfen
obviously	offensichtlich
rather	eher, ziemlich
violent	gewalttätig, brutal
to remember sth.	sich erinnern an
involved	verwickelt, involviert

Sunderland in the North-East of England. "The Village Fair" or "The Village Fête" seems to be a very middle-class topic. Typical for the South Coast!

"Rose, that's not easy. I'll manage somehow – but what about Jim?"

Rose turns to Jim Ryan, pauses and takes a deep breath.

"Jim, you know Church Hill's motto. 'Learning by Doing'. We want to change it a little for your theme. You should produce a short drama with the title 'Learning by Killing'. So, it's **obviously** a **rather violent** play. But **remember** – it is a play! We don't want the local police **involved**!"

The four teachers smile and laugh a little. Jim Ryan looks
around.

"Rose, all of you. I come from Ireland. That means I know
all about violence, **murder**, and so on. Not personally, of
course. But I think, with a little bit of **imagination**, I can
produce a short play. Dramatic but short! It **depends on**
the students I have, naturally."

The others clap their hands. Rose's mobile rings.

"Ah, there's the boss-man. My father's ringing to find out
whether everything's going **smoothly**. OK. **Let's call it a day**. See
you all tomorrow. Remember! Monday, 9 a.m. sharp!"

The teachers for the Summer School of 2017 collect their notes,
smiling, laughing and ready to start teaching.

Later, at the harbour, Tracy finishes painting the mast. She
looks up at the cliffs. On the highest cliff, she sees the castle.
It must be at least 800 years
old. The stone is grey but, in
the sunlight, now seems very
white. The seagulls are still
screeching.

And this is England, she thinks.
The England I love. And Jim
Ryan? He's not English –
he's Irish. But that doesn't
matter.

murder	Mord
imagination	Fantasie; Vorstel-lung
to depend on	abhängen von
smoothly	problemlos, rei-bungslos
Let's call it a day.	Machen wir Schluss (für heute).

Tracy goes back to her car, singing a well-known sea shanty quietly to herself.

"Where have you been all the day, Billy Boy, Billy Boy, where have you been all the day, my Billy Boy? Oh, I've been walking

sea shanty	Seemannslied
⚡ to tickle sb.'s fancy	jdn. reizen
to set	*hier*: untergehen
Channel	Ärmelkanal
tranquillity	Stille

all the day with my darling Nancy Grey, and my Nancy tickled my fancy, oh my darling Nancy Grey."

Billy Boy and Nancy Grey, she thinks. Or Jimmy Ryan and Tracy Dean?

The sun begins to set on Eastcastle. The English Channel shimmers in the background. One of the large Dover car ferries, a speck on the horizon, is moving slowly towards France. Four or five yachts are returning to the harbour after a day's sailing. The weather forecast is positive. Can anything, anything at all, disturb this tranquillity?

2 Departure Lounge

"Good morning, ladies and gentlemen!"

Jim Ryan sees five students sitting in the room. Two men and three women. They're all a little nervous in their first lesson.

Pierre Leclerc is talking to Elke, a young lady from Zurich. Elke has long blond hair, very large blue eyes and a **figure** that Pierre is **familiar with** from magazines. Pierre is certain that Elke is a model who needs to learn English. He smiles at her and shakes his head of dark hair.

figure	*hier*: Gestalt; Figur
familiar (with)	vertraut (mit), sich auskennen (mit)
biro	Kugelschreiber
briefcase	Aktentasche
proudly	stolz
to adjust sth.	etw. zurechtrücken

Karl Schultze is sitting at his desk. In front of him, he has a folder, two pencils and a **biro**. The biro is blue – not black and not red. His dictionary is in his **briefcase**, which stands **proudly** next to the desk. Karl **adjusts**[i] his glasses and looks at Mr Ryan, ready and waiting.

Ein kleiner Tipp:
Nutzen Sie bereits bekannte Wörter, um unbekannte Vokabeln herzuleiten. Manchmal helfen dabei auch Fremdwörter im Deutschen weiter: **to adjust** „zurechtrücken, gerade rücken" ist verwandt mit dem deutschen „justieren".

Next to him is Franca from Spain. A very beautiful woman – with red hair! A redhead! From Spain? Yes, indeed. She can't speak English very well, but she can produce a beautiful "th" – the others always

splutter, particularly Karl. The fifth student is Mahdi. He comes from Oman. He's not interested in the girls, the women, the ladies! He wants to learn English. He wants to be **successful** and develop his country. English! THE language! The "lingua franca" of globalisation. Or is it globalization? He **makes a mental note** to ask the teacher later.

Jim Ryan stands in front of the class. He pauses, and then he says:

to splutter	hervorstoßen, stammeln
successful	erfolgreich
to make a mental note of sth.	sich etw. merken
to bow	(sich) verbeugen
modestly	bescheiden
blank	*hier*: verständnislos, leer

"My name is Jim. Jim Ryan. And what's your name?"

He goes round the class. They all introduce themselves. Pierre gives his name and laughs. Karl gives his name and stares. Elke and Franca say their names very clearly. Mahdi is the only person who introduces himself formally.

"Teacher, I am Mahdi – from Oman. My country needs people who speak good English. I am here to learn English. I like fish and chips. Thank you very much."

Mahdi **bows modestly** and sits down.

Jim Ryan opens his notebook. "So, we have a Pierre, a Karl, an Elke, a Franca and a Mahdi. That's good, very good. Does anyone know why?"

His students look at him with **blank** faces.

"OK, I'll tell you why. We're going to learn English in the next three weeks. 'Learning by Doing' is the motto of Church Hill School. And we, you five students and myself, are going to produce a play. Not a comedy, not a tragedy – just a simple murder story. 'Learning by Doing' may be the motto of Church Hill, but the title of our little play is 'Learning by Killing'!"

Exercise 4: Unscramble the definitions. Enträtseln Sie die folgenden Definitionen!

1. A newspaper with lots of pictures: agzanemi

_____

2. A small table where you can work: edks _____

3. Something you can write with: oibr _____

4. A bag for carrying papers and books: sefibcrae

_____

5. Something you organize your papers in: rlfdoe

_____

6. Pieces of fried potato: ichsp _____

7. A person with red hair: ahddeer _____

8. A group of pupils or students who are taught and

study together: saslc _____

Jim Ryan begins to hand out some sheets of paper.

"Now, I know that all of you have about two or three years of English behind you. That means that we have to keep the dialogue in this play fairly simple. Its **success** depends on... Yes, Mahdi?", Jim Ryan looks at the young man. "You've got a question. That's good. Any questions – just ask!"

Mahdi is **slightly embarrassed**. He's not sure what the word "dialogue" really means. He

success	Erfolg
slightly	etwas, ein bisschen
embarrassed	verlegen

knows the verb "to die", and he also knows that "a log" is a piece of wood. You can put logs on a fire. But "dialogue"? Karl picks up his biro and opens his notebook. Pierre laughs again and looks once more at Elke. He knows all about dialogues, especially dialogues with beautiful Swiss women.

Jim Ryan explains enthusiastically:

Exercise 5: Verb forms. Lesen Sie weiter und setzen Sie die richtige Verbform ein!

"A dialogue, Mahdi, **1.** be _____ when two people talk to each other. At the moment, I **2.** talk _____ to you, and I **3.** try _____ to tell you what this word **4.** mean _____. Now you can tell me that you understand the meaning of the word. OK?"

Mahdi **5.** nod _____ his head but **6.** say _____ nothing.

Jim Ryan asks once more: "Do you understand the meaning of 'dialogue' now?"

Mahdi waves his hands and grins. "Dialogue," he says. "OK, two people talking to each other – like in the movies." He **emphasizes** the word "movies".

Karl Schultze carefully writes the word "movies" next to the word "dialogue" and then **adds** a question mark. He must check

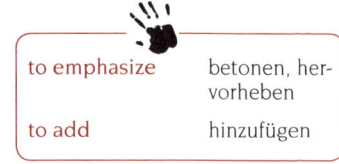

| to emphasize | betonen, hervorheben |
| to add | hinzufügen |

this when he goes back to his bed and breakfast[i] **accommodation**.

"Exactly," says Jim Ryan. "But this is not a movie, Mahdi. This is a play. For us the dialogue is in the play. Now, look at your sheets of paper. There are five characters in this short play. I think we can use your real names. The play has got two scenes. The first scene takes place in a small studio, well, a **bedsit** really, and there are two actors, let's say Karl and Franca. Karl is an artist, and Franca is his model. In the beginning, a business relationship, but now they are lovers."

Mahdi and Karl **exchange** glances. This word sounds **suspicious**.

"Karl, however, has a **patroness**. That will be you, Elke. You are much older than Karl, and you are a very **jealous** woman."

At this point, Elke closes her dictionary, very loudly.

"Jim, Mr Ryan, this is not true. I am not jealous. Nobody in Switzerland is jealous of other people. Other people are jealous of the Swiss. We have got the mountains, the lakes – and the Swiss Franc!"

"Yes, Elke, you're quite right, of course. But don't forget that the Swiss Franc is a kind of money. In Britain, we think the Swiss Franc is cold and antiseptic. We think that the Swiss are people who show no emotions. Let's see – do you know what the difference between heaven and hell is?"

The students are quiet again and listen **attentively**.

accommodation	Unterkunft
bedsit	möbliertes Zimmer, Einzimmerwohnung
to exchange	wechseln, austauschen
suspicious	misstrauisch; verdächtig
patroness	Mäzenin
jealous	eifersüchtig
attentively	aufmerksam

"In hell," Jim explains, "the English are the cooks, the Germans are the police, the French are the mechanics, the Swiss are the lovers, and the Spanish are the bankers."

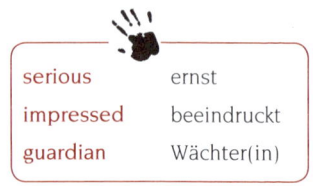

serious	ernst
impressed	beeindruckt
guardian	Wächter(in)

Jim Ryan pauses dramatically. Nobody laughs except Mahdi. Elke looks very unhappy. Pierre tries to give moral support with his dark brown eyes. He smoothes back his long black hair and looks very serious. The other two, Karl and Franca, aren't sure if this is a joke.

"In heaven, on the other hand," Jim Ryan continues, "the English are the police, the Germans are the mechanics, the French are the cooks, the Swiss are the bankers, and the Spanish are the lovers. You see, that's the difference between heaven and hell."

Mahdi raises his hand. "Teacher, Mr Jim Ryan, what about the Omanis?"

Then Franca raises her hand. "Jim, where are the Irish in this little story?" She smiles sweetly.

Jim Ryan is impressed. They understand the story. They understand the humour.

"Well, if you must know... hmmm... the Omanis are the guardians of heaven and, well, the Irish must be the guardians of hell."

Everybody laughs. They are beginning to relax. Jim Ryan hands out some more sheets.

"Now, the second scene is in a pub – you all know what a pub is, of course."

Karl raises his hand, removes his glasses and says very seriously: "A pub, Mr Ryan, is a building where people go to drink and meet their friends. Pubs serve alcoholic and other drinks, and often also food."

"Excellent, Karl," says Jim Ryan, "that's an excellent definition. How do you know that?"

Karl Schultze blushes and then puts his glasses back on. He picks up the dictionary.

"It is here, Mr Ryan, in this dictionary." He pronounces the word "dictionary" very slowly, very carefully with an air of triumph.

Jim Ryan raises both thumbs in appreciation. "Yes, the dictionary. Have you all got a dictionary?"

Three students look in their briefcases. One student grins and does nothing. This, of course, is Pierre Leclerc. He's a Frenchman. Like all Frenchmen, he thinks that the English language is really French. All you need to do is to speak French with an English accent. Voilà – or, in English 'There you are!' Easy, isn't it?

"Brilliant," says Jim Ryan.

to blush	rot werden, erröten
appreciation	Anerkennung
upset	aufgeregt, verärgert
praise	Lob
⚡ to send daggers	tödliche Blicke zuwerfen
direction	Richtung
to smirk	süffisant lächeln
witty	geistreich, witzig
handsome	gutaussehend
passionately	leidenschaftlich

"Pierre, I see that you haven't got a dictionary. Buy one, as soon as possible! You'll need it! And Karl, remember that we use first names here. My name is Jim, short for James. Now, let's talk about the second scene of our play."

Karl is slightly upset and a little embarrassed. First you get praise; then you get criticism. These English, they're so unfair! Pierre is angry. His dark brown eyes send daggers in the direction of Jim Ryan. Elke smirks, and Franca claps her hands. Jim, she thinks. Jim Ryan – yes, you are a very witty, clever and handsome man.

Jim carries on. "Elke and Pierre are sitting in the pub. Elke is passionately in love with Karl, the artist – she's older than he is – and she knows that Karl is having an affair with his model

Franca. Elke feels betrayed. After all, she pays the bills for this artistic genius and wants something more than just paintings in return. She decides that Karl must die."

"This is a very drastic decision," Jim explains. "She will lose the young man she is in love with, and the world will lose a potentially great artist. But there we are – jealousy is an uncontrollable passion. She hires Pierre, a professional killer, who shoots Karl."

Karl nods his head slowly. He likes the idea. And the more he thinks about it, the more he likes it. He has an affair with two women in this play. Both are very attractive. He cleans his glasses and focuses on the redhead from Spain. He is beginning to enjoy this three-week stay in Eastcastle, with opportunities that he never thought about before in Gifhorn.

"Jim," Mahdi says shyly, but with more confidence than before, "Jim, what is my role in the play? I cannot possibly be the barman. I'm a Muslim."

betrayed	betrogen; verraten
to hire	einstellen, anheuern
stay	Aufenthalt
opportunity	Gelegenheit, Möglichkeit
shyly	schüchtern
confidence	(Selbst-)Vertrauen, Zuversicht
innocent	unschuldig; ahnungslos
witness	Zeuge, Zeugin
corpse	Leiche
to remind sb. (of sth.)	jdn. (an etw.) erinnern

"All very simple, Mahdi. You are an innocent witness, and you discover the corpse."

Mahdi likes the sound of the word "corpse". It reminds him of "cops". This is a very good role in the play. He lowers his head, closes his eyes and puts his hands together. He is very proud and remembers a phrase from the Christian Bible and says: "Thy will be done, on earth as in heaven."

The others laugh, and Jim is happy that the ice is broken. Even Elke is giggling. Pierre points two fingers and a thumb

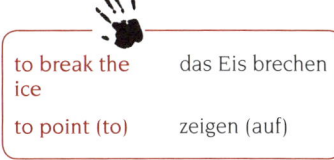

| to break the ice | das Eis brechen |
| to point (to) | zeigen (auf) |

at Jim Ryan and says, "Bang, bang". Franca looks at Karl, who is making more notes.

Yes, she thinks, he's rather short and rather plump, and I hope I don't have to kiss him – but, after all, it is only a play.

Exercise 6: Word order. Wie lauten die Wörter in der richtigen Reihenfolge?

1. you   put   can   on   fire   logs   a

_____

2. picks   Karl   biro   his   up

_____

3. with   French   speaks   accent   Pierre   a

_____

4. pub   in   meet   people   friends   their   a

_____

5. Karl   die   that   must   decides   she

_____

6. witness   an   are   innocent   you

_____

7. broken   happy   is   ice   Jim   is   that   the

_____

It's Sunday, and there are five days left until the play **is performed**. Jim and Tracy are down at the harbour, enjoying the sunset. Their affair is now five weeks old. Tracy is throwing a few **pebbles** into the water, wondering how she can turn the conversation to the future – that is, if there is a future for her with Jim Ryan.

to be performed	aufgeführt werden
pebble	Kieselstein
bright	intelligent
tax-free	steuerfrei
allowance	*hier*: Beihilfe, Zulage
ties *pl*	Bindungen
to hand in one's notice	kündigen

"Jim," she smiles. "I want to talk about us. You must know that I'm very much in love with you. What I need to know is where I stand and where you stand in this relationship."

Jim looks out to the sea and shrugs his shoulders. "What can I say? You're a wonderful woman, Tracy. You're very attractive, you're great fun, and you're **bright**. But – I'm the wrong person for you. My contract finishes next week, the day after the final presentations. And then I'll move on. In fact, I've already got another teaching post. The chance of a lifetime. A five-year contract in the Middle East – **tax-free**, overseas **allowance** plus marriage and family allowance plus..."

Tracy laughs happily and says: "Why, Jim, that sounds marvellous. OK, I love Eastcastle, but I've got no real **ties** here. Well, except for the yacht, but I can easily sell that. And I only rent the flat. Where is the contract exactly?"

"If you must know, it's Saudi Arabia, teaching Business English to Saudis in one of the big oil companies. But Tracy, I don't think

Flat ist das britische Wort für „Wohnung", während Amerikaner hierzu **apartment** sagen.

you quite understand what I'm trying to say."

In her mind, Tracy is already planning how she can **hand in** her notice to the school and her landlord. That won't be a problem. In fact, she could leave within a couple of weeks, and she knows that her neighbour is looking for a yacht just like hers. She laughs happily and pulls at Jim's arm.

"Oh, Jim. Don't make things so complicated. I can join you after you move in. Saudi Arabia sounds wonderful. OK, it may be a little hot, but I'm sure I can find some sort of secretarial work. Why are you telling me this only now? It's too good to be true!"

landlord	Vermieter; Gastwirt
to glow	leuchten
to cast	*hier*: werfen
shadow	Schatten
to envelop	einhüllen
to shiver	zittern
to scramble	stürzen, hasten
impostor	Betrüger(in)

For a few seconds a cloud covers the setting sun, and the horizon begins to glow pink and red. Jim turns and stands in front of Tracy. His silhouette casts a long black shadow that envelops Tracy totally.

"There's something you should know, Tracy. I'm a married man. I've got two children. The plan is that they join me in Riad in September. Church Hill is just a temporary post. I'm sorry. I'm afraid you and I have no future, none at all."

As the sun reappears, Tracy stands up. Her face says everything. She is shocked. So shocked that she begins to shiver, although a warm breeze is blowing off the Channel.

"But the last five weeks – last Thursday – last Monday. Does all that mean nothing? You said that..."

"I know, I know. This is all my fault. I'm an impulsive bastard. I always involve innocent people. I'm sorry. This, here, is the end for us."

Tracy scrambles off the beach towards her car. She is heartbroken. What a fool she is. She loves someone who is already married with two children. The impostor!

She turns round and screams at Jim: "Is this really true!? You flirt with me, you invite me out for drinks and dinner, you make love to me, you even tell me you love me. And all the time

shame	Scham, Schande
actor/ actress *m/f*	Schauspieler(in)
kind	Art, Sorte
⚡ to roar off	davondonnern

you're a married man. How can you do this to me?"

Jim looks into the distance. Perhaps he feels some **shame**, because he answers in a very deep voice. But then Jim is a very good **actor**.

"I'm sorry, Tracy. I'm afraid, this is the end of our affair."

Tracy tries to control herself. "You know what? You're not an impulsive bastard, Jim. You are a total bastard. A bastard of the worst **kind**. Don't ever speak to me again!"

Tracy runs off to the car, gets in and **roars off**. Jim kicks a few pebbles, puts his hands in his pockets and walks to the nearest pub.

Exercise 7: True or false? Welche der folgenden Aussagen sind wahr? Markieren Sie mit richtig ✔ oder falsch – !

1. Jim and Tracy meet at the harbour early in the morning. ☐

2. Jim thinks Tracy is very stupid. ☐

3. Jim has got a contract in Singapore for five years. ☐

4. Tracy can hand in her notice to her landlord quite quickly. ☐

5. Tracy does not want to move to Saudi Arabia. ☐

6. Jim Ryan has got three children. ☐

7. It is quite warm at the harbour. ☐

3 Departure

On Thursday of their third week, Class B1 is word perfect in the two scenes of the play. They know the dialogue by heart. They're all enjoying themselves and are now very relaxed in each other's company. Elke really wants to play the part of the older patroness and is experimenting with make-up and a

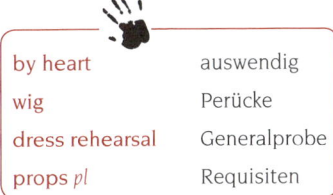

by heart	auswendig
wig	Perücke
dress rehearsal	Generalprobe
props *pl*	Requisiten

couple of wigs from the local Amateur Dramatic Society. Pierre is very enthusiastic about his part. As the murderer, he must appear totally cool. He must be a professional and mustn't show any emotions. This could be difficult for a Frenchman – but, after all, it is only a play. Karl is happy. He can finally show everyone that under his North German exterior he actually ⓘ is a romantic artist, a man with passion. Franca is now quite happy to be Karl's model. She doesn't have to take off her clothes, and she doesn't have to kiss Karl. Mahdi goes back to his bed and breakfast every day and thanks Allah that he is simply an innocent witness. And he's learning English very fast, which pleases him.

Actually wird häufig falsch verwendet. Auch wenn es an das deutsche „aktuell" erinnert, bedeutet es doch „tatsächlich", „eigentlich". „Aktuell", „derzeitig" kann z. B. mit dem Adverb **currently** übersetzt werden: *The teacher is **currently** unavailable.*

After the dress rehearsal, the players collect all their papers and props and leave for the pub.

Jim Ryan stays in the school. He has something important to do. He knocks at the door of Colonel Lessons's office, **whistling** an old Irish folk song and **feels** totally **at ease**. The "Tracy thing" is over. The B1 class are absolutely marvellous, and he knows that the performance on Friday will be a great success. The contract for Saudi Arabia is signed and ready to be posted. Of course he's not married! Two children? What a crazy idea!

"Come in!" shouts Colonel Lessons.

Jim Ryan opens the door.

"Ah, Jim. Sit yourself down. Everything OK? Any problems? Would you like a whiskey – it's Irish, you know."

The Colonel reaches up to a shelf and takes down a **volume** of the Oxford English Dictionary. He puts it upright on the table, opens one side and takes out a small **hip flask**. He

to whistle	pfeifen
to feel at ease	sich wohl fühlen
volume	*hier*: Band, Buch
hip flask	Flachmann
to suspect	verdächtigen
dedicated	engagiert
to get sth. off one's chest	sich etw. von der Seele reden

smiles. He's dreaming about the South of France, and he **suspects** that Jim Ryan wants his salary before the contract finishes. No way! Ryan is a very good teacher, but he has to wait four weeks!

Jim folds his hands very modestly. "No thanks, Colonel," he says, "I still have to do some work on the presentation. Last minute changes."

The Colonel grins. This man is **dedicated**! He pours himself a large glass of whiskey. Perhaps Majorca would be better than Cannes? He looks at Jim and waits.

"Fire away, young man! **Get it off your chest**!"

"Well, Colonel. My contract finishes on Saturday, as you well know."

Colonel Lessons nods his head **encouragingly**.

"The thing is," Jim says, "I need some money, quite a large amount of money, before I take up my next job. And I think you can give it to me."

A long silence follows. Colonel Lessons takes a **gulp** of whiskey and almost **chokes**. The **impertinence**! The **fellow** really does want payment in advance! These Irish are so **cocky**!

"I'm not sure what you're getting at, Ryan," the Colonel says. Jim **settles back** in the chair and takes out a notebook.

"Colonel, just listen to the notes I have here," he goes on. "You charge £800 per student for a course of three weeks. You

encouragingly	ermutigend
gulp	(großer) Schluck
to choke	ersticken; würgen
impertinence	Frechheit, Dreistigkeit
fellow	Kerl, Bursche
⚡ cocky	großspurig, frech
to settle back	sich zurücklehnen

pay the teacher £600 pounds for three weeks. You get a 20% cut from the bed and breakfast accommodation. You pick up 10% from the two pubs where the students drink. You give the students mock certificates for completing the course. You aren't even registered with any of the agencies that control courses for teaching English as a foreign language. In fact, Church Hill School for English is a gold mine and, at the moment, all the gold goes to you."

cut	*hier*: Anteil, Provision
white as a sheet	kreidebleich
fireproof	brandsicher, feuerfest
under false pretences	unter Vorspiegelung falscher Tatsachen
blackmail	Erpressung
to report	melden, berichten; anzeigen
mist	Nebel

The Colonel is as white as a sheet. He takes another gulp of whiskey. Jim Ryan stands up and looks around.

"This building isn't fireproof. There are no escape routes from upstairs. You even illegally employ Polish migrants to do the repairs. All in all, you are making a great deal of money under false pretences."

The Colonel finishes his whiskey and pours another. His voice is now very loud. "This is blackmail, Ryan! Everything you say may be true. But – and it's a big but – it may NOT be true. Now, you're a man of business. What do you really want?"

Jim Ryan's answer is calm and cool: "Colonel, I can report all of this tomorrow to the Ministry of Education or the Department of Health and Safety. Then you're ruined. Am I right – or, am I right?" There is a long pause as the Colonel thinks. He sees Majorca sinking, the South of France disappearing in a mist.

"How much?" he asks

Jim Ryan grins, sits down and crosses his legs. He puts the notebook into his pocket.

"30 grand, Colonel. That's a bargain. I leave for Saudi Arabia on Sunday. Give me the money at the station, and then everything's OK."

The Colonel hesitates. He tries to work out the price of property between Cannes and Calais.

"20," he says, in a very military tone.

⚡ grand	tausend Pfund
bargain	günstiges Angebot, Schnäppchen
property	*hier*: Immobilien
envelope	Briefumschlag
vigorously	energisch, kräftig
to dial	wählen

Ryan smiles. "OK, let's make it 25. Sunday, at the station, used notes in a brown envelope."

Jim Ryan stands up and holds out his hand. Colonel Lessons shakes it vigorously.

"You're a bastard, Ryan. Now get out!"

As soon as Jim leaves the office, Lessons dials Tracy's number.

"Tracy! We need some cash, fairly quickly. I'll give you the details tomorrow, but we're talking about 25,000. That's possible, isn't it?"

"Of course, Colonel. What's wrong?"

Exercise 9: Synonyms. Welche Wörter haben eine ähnliche Bedeutung? Ordnen Sie zu!

1. cocky	☐	energetically
2. cut	☐	relaxed
3. hip flask	☐	impertinent
4. under false pretences	☐	thousand
5. calm	☐	commission
6. grand	☐	bottle
7. vigorously	☐	illegally

Colonel Lessons tries to pour another whisky, but the hip flask is now empty.

"Nothing, Tracy. Nothing at all. We'll sort it out tomorrow. Just take the money out of the bank and keep it in your flat till Sunday."

Friday is the day of the presentations. The four groups are all ready and waiting. Janet's group starts at 10 in the morning. They sing traditional songs like "Greensleeves", but also have a Karaoke session. Pat's

to sort sth. out	etw. regeln
in charge (of)	verantwortlich, zuständig (für); leiten
bangers and mash	Würstchen mit Kartoffelbrei
toad-in-the-hole	in Teig gebackene Würstchen
shepherd's pie	Auflauf aus Hackfleisch und Kartoffelbrei
hall	*hier:* Saal
to look forward to	sich freuen auf
to disappear	verschwinden
curtain	Vorhang
audience	Publikum

group organizes various activities in the back garden: a traditional English Fête – the sack race is a great success. The third group, with Terry in charge, produces a midday meal. The students can choose from bangers and mash, toad-in-the-hole or shepherd's pie. They can also drink "Real Ale," traditional English beer. This item on the menu, however, is not very popular, particularly with the Japanese students.

At 3 p.m., it's the turn of Jim Ryan's group. Everybody goes into the main hall, a large room with a stage at the back. Here they all sit down in a sort of circle. The students are laughing and talking, some in their own language, but most of them in English. They're very pleased with their progress and are looking forward to the final presentation. Jim, Elke, Franca, Karl, Mahdi and Pierre walk to the front and disappear behind a large curtain. Karl steps out and talks to the audience.

"Ladies and gentlemen, it is our pleasure to present a short play. Look, please, at your programme. You all know the motto of

Church Hill School, namely 'Learning by Doing', but the title of our play is 'Learning by Killing'. This is an example of English irony."

The students **chuckle** and begin to **clap**. Karl is **sweating** but very happy that they like his joke. He continues.

"The plot is simple. Love, **betrayal**, jealousy and murder. I hope that you enjoy our little play. The text, by the way, is included in your programme."

to chuckle	kichern, in sich hineinlachen
to clap	klatschen
to sweat	schwitzen
betrayal	Verrat
awkwardly	ungeschickt
to recognize	erkennen
canvas	Leinwand
convincing	überzeugend
setting	Schauplatz

Karl bows rather **awkwardly**, holding his glasses, and then disappears backstage. The curtain is drawn back. The students smile and begin to clap again. Jim Ryan and his team have created an authentic flat with props. Most students **recognize** the sort of bedsit that they live in. They see a bed, a table, two chairs, a wash basin but also **canvasses** and half-finished paintings.

In the short first scene, Karl and Franca are very **convincing**. All the students understand that passion plays an important role in this little play.

Die fantasievollen Namen der Pubs in Großbritannien gehen zurück auf Zeiten, in denen weite Teile der Bevölkerung noch nicht lesen und schreiben konnten. Die meisten Pubnamen erinnern an historische Ereignisse. Tier- oder Pflanzennamen gehen meist auf lokale Wappen zurück. Der mit Abstand häufigste Pubname ist **The Red Lion.**

They now know that something "dramatic" will happen in the second scene. After the curtain is opened again, there is even more applause.

This time the **setting** is a pub. It looks just like the "The Cherry Tree," [i] the pub where most of the students spend their evenings. It's only two hundred metres from the school. Of course, they don't know that Colonel Lessons has "an arrangement" with the landlord. Ten per cent! There are several comfortable chairs and a table as the bar, with pieces painted to look like dark, Victorian wood. Lots of glasses hanging upside down and bottles behind, also upside down. Music is playing quietly in the background. Elke and Pierre are sitting at a table, whispering. The students study the text in the programme.

⚡ tiff	Geplänkel, kleiner Streit
solution	Lösung
to apologize	(sich) entschuldigen
temptation	Versuchung
wrinkle	(Gesichts-)Falte
to offer	(an)bieten

E: So, Pierre, you know what to do. Have you got the gun?

P: Do you want to see it? I can show it to you.

E: Not here, you fool. People may be looking at us. You know the plan. I have an argument with Karl. A lovers' **tiff**, as they say. I tell him that I know he is having an affair – an affair with that silly young woman, Franca.

I leave and go to the car park. He follows me. I know he will. He wants my money and my contacts. I drive away, and then you shoot. It's all a great tragedy, and the world will lose a great artist. But there is no other **solution**. Think of... Aaah, here he comes!

Pierre moves to another table when Karl enters the pub. Karl **apologizes** for being late and sits in a chair. Then he tells Elke all about Franca, how pretty she is, much prettier than his previous model.

The audience smile and chuckle. Dramatic irony. They already know much more about what is happening than Karl does.

Then Karl says that he wants to give his new painting the title "Temptation". There is a long pause. Then Elke takes out a mirror and looks at her wrinkles.

E: Oh, sweet bird of youth! And I am so old and wrinkled and tired. I have nothing to offer anymore.

K: Now, Elke. You know that that's simply not true. You're the most beautiful woman in the world. You are my muse, you are my inspiration, my sun and my moon – and you are also the love of my life!

The audience cannot help laughing. After all, Elke, despite her make-up, is a very attractive woman, and Karl – well, Karl is rather short and plump. And he wears glasses. Elke continues.

E: Thank you, Karl. But that's not enough. I may be the love of your life but you don't really love ME! You only love my money! You're only interested in me because I pay your bills! Listen, I know what's going on. I know you are having an affair with this woman, this girl. So we must end our affairs, both of them. The sexual affair... and the business affair!

Exercise 10: Simple present or present continuous?
Lesen Sie weiter und setzen Sie die Verben in der richtigen Form ein!

K: Don't say that, Elke! I love you more than words can say. I **1.** think _____ of you every minute of the day.

E: We are finished. Goodbye!

Elke **2.** leave _____. Karl, **stunned**, sits for a moment longer and then **3.** run _____ out. Pierre **4.** hurry _____ to the door and **5.** follow _____ him. A shot is heard in the background. Suddenly Mahdi appears.

M: Help! Call the police. Call an ambulance. A man **6.** lie _____ in the car park! I think he **7.** die _____.

Mahdi exits and returns a few moments later. He raises his hands and looks at the audience.

M: The man is dead. This is a terrible tragedy. His last words were "Elke, Franca, temptation". May he rest in peace.

The curtain is drawn, and the students of Church Hill School begin to applaud. Colonel Lessons appears from the front of the hall, marches to the stage and then turns to the audience. They clap their hands, louder and louder. What a superb end to three weeks in Eastcastle. All the presentations. Food, songs, village life!
The players step round the curtain, holding hands. Elke bows first, and the others follow. They are all smiling, pleased that the production is so successful. Karl polishes his glasses, raises his arms in triumph and then waves his hands to silence the audience. He's absolutely thrilled.

"Ladies and gentlemen," he says. "Thank you for your appreciation. You obviously liked our little play. Now we must give thanks to our teacher, director and producer – Jim Ryan!! Jim, please come out!"

Karl turns to the curtain, but nothing happens.

The students continue to clap – and clap – and clap. Nobody appears. Karl whispers to Mahdi, ⓘ

> Anders als im Deutschen werden Relativsätze nur dann mit einem Komma vom Bezugswort abgetrennt, wenn sie eine zusätzliche Information enthalten und das Bezugswort nicht definieren.
> *Karl whispers to **Mahdi, who** then disappears.*
> Aber: *Tracy loves **someone who** is already married.*

who then disappears behind the curtain. The clap becomes a slow handclap. Everybody is waiting for Jim Ryan.

Suddenly Mahdi runs through the curtain, pulling it down and knocking over several of the props. He's frantic. He turns to the

stunned	benommen; fassungslos
to rest in peace	in Frieden ruhen
to silence	zum Schweigen bringen
thrilled	begeistert, hingerissen
to knock over	umwerfen, umstoßen
frantic	völlig verzweifelt
to wonder	sich fragen
grimly	grimmig, streng
to scream	schreien, kreischen

players and then to the audience. He raises his hands and begins to cry.

The students begin to sit down. Is this part of the play? they wonder.

Mahdi turns to Pierre and whispers something. Pierre marches forward. He looks at the audience grimly.

"Something is very wrong here. Sacre-bleu! Jim Ryan is dead. Please leave the room. This is not a play. Jim Ryan, our teacher, is dead!"

The curtain closes again. Some of the younger students begin to scream.

Exercise 11: Translation. Übersetzen Sie folgende Sätze ins Deutsche!

1. They are ready to present their tasks.

   _____

2. The students are laughing and talking.

   _____

3. They are looking forward to the presentation.

   _____

4. Mahdi disappears behind the curtain.

   _____

5. I drive away and then you shoot.

   _____

6. Karl polishes his glasses.

   _____

7. Some students begin to cry.

   _____

4. Left Luggage

Inspector Watson from the local police is tired. It's Saturday morning, and the temperature is already around 30 degrees. But he must continue with the interviews. Most of the students want to leave on Sunday. The five members of Jim Ryan's class are extremely upset and can give no useful information. The revolver from the play is on the desk in front of him. It's plastic, of course, and cannot be used to kill anyone.

Pierre still has the **receipt** from the local toyshop – £5.50. Watson also has the first report from **forensics**. This says that the murderer must have shot Ryan from a corner

receipt	Quittung
forensics	Kriminal-technik

behind the stage, probably the left-hand corner, because that's where the door to the back garden is. The murderer must be familiar with guns. After all, the distance from the door to Ryan's body is about 10 metres.

The next student, a young man from Terry's class, knocks and enters the room.

"Ah, let's see." Watson looks at his list. "You must be Mr Olsen, from Denmark, I think."

"That's right, Inspector. How can I help?"

"Well, according to my plan here, your seat was in the second row, the last one on the right-hand side, so perhaps you could actually see this door which leads into the garden?"

Jens Olsen smiles and says:

Exercise 12: Simple past. Lesen Sie weiter und setzen Sie die Verben in der passenden Verbform ein!

"I understand, Inspector. Now let me think back." He concentrates. "The play **1.** be _____ great fun. The actors **2.** be _____ superb. Very good English. We **3.** understand _____ everything. After Elke **4.** leave _____ the pub, the audience were all very quiet. We **5.** know _____ that something was going to happen, a fight or a murder. When the gun **went off**, there was some laughter – we all knew it was a toy gun. And I can tell you this. After the shot, I **6.** hear _____ three sounds very clearly. One was a cry of pain. Well, we **7.** think _____ that was part of the play."

"Go on," says Inspector Watson softly.

"The second was a **thud** – is that what you say in English?" Watson looks up from his notebook and nods.

"It was like a body that falls to the ground," the young man continues. "Or the floor. The main hall has wooden floorboards. And then, in the total silence before the applause, I heard that someone **slammed** a door. It must be this door on your plan. So the killer left the main hall by this door – is that what you think?"

to go off	*hier*: losgehen
thud	dumpfes Geräusch
to slam	zuschlagen, zuknallen

"Thank you, Mr Olsen. Very helpful. When do you return to Denmark?" Watsons asks.

"Monday, Inspector. From Heathrow to Kastrup, that's the airport
in Copenhagen."

strange	merkwürdig, seltsam
unsolved	ungelöst
to mop	wischen
investigation	Ermittlung, Untersuchung

When Jens Olsen has left the room, Watson leans back in his chair. So! His hypothesis is correct. The killer shot from behind and exited into the garden. But who is the killer? And where is the weapon? And what is the motive? Questions, questions – and no answers!

The interviews continue. After the students, the teachers – and then, finally, the staff. Rose can give no helpful information. She was there at the performance but saw and heard nothing strange. Tracy was at home. She always has Friday afternoons free. The last person to come in is Mrs Bradley, the cleaner. Inspector Watson begins to feel that this case may remain unsolved. It could be "the perfect murder".

"Sit down, Mrs Bradley. Now, I wonder if you can tell me why someone wanted to kill Jim Ryan?"

"Well, Inspector, I'm not really sure. I mean, perhaps it's nothing important – but on Thursday evening, when I started to mop the floor..."

While Inspector Watson is doing his interviews, Colonel Lessons is at Number 19. He's happy that he doesn't need to be at Church Hill until the late afternoon. Tracy is organizing everything, and Rose is there, too. He orders another gin and tonic and smiles at the barmaid.

Well, he thinks, that's all over. Jim Ryan's dead. No investigations from the Ministry of Education. OK, those students from the B1 class are rather upset, and one or two others may miss their flights back home. Perhaps I'll lower their fees – say £50 –

and then everything will be forgotten. An unfortunate incident. Very unfortunate for Jim Ryan!

Exercise 13: Questions about the text. Beantworten Sie folgende Fragen auf Englisch!

1. Why can Ryan's class give no useful information?

   _____

2. How much did the toy gun cost?

   _____

3. Where was Olsen's seat?

   _____

4. How many sounds did Olsen hear?

   _____

5. Where was Tracy on Friday?

   _____

6. What is the cleaner's name?

   _____

7. Where does Olsen live?

   _____

The Colonel, a military man through and through, turns to the collection of antique guns behind the bar.

"Judy, tell me. That collection behind you. Do all those guns still work?"

The barmaid shrugs her shoulders and pours another pint of beer.

"Colonel, to be honest, I've no idea," she says. "They belong to the Secretary of the Golf Club. He's a collector, you know. But why don't you ask Tracy Dean. She was the barmaid here before me. She'll know. Another gin and tonic, Colonel?"

incident	Zwischenfall, Ereignis
to sip	nippen
confident	*hier*: zuversichtlich
to solve	lösen
to loosen one's collar	den Kragen lockern
to afford	sich leisten

"Yes, of course! I'm feeling lucky today!"

While the Colonel is **sipping** his gin and tonic, the phone rings. Judy picks it up. After a few seconds, she turns to Lessons.

"It's the police, Colonel. An Inspector Watson. He wants to see you down at the school – immediately!"

"Damn!" says Lessons. "OK, Judy, tell him I'm on my way."

The Colonel gulps the rest of his drink and heads out to the Rolls Royce.

Inspector Watson is now very **confident** that he can **solve** the murder. He **loosens his collar**. When Colonel Lessons comes in, he writes the time in his notebook: 15:34.

"Colonel, how good of you to come so quickly. No problems, I hope."

The Colonel is extremely angry.

"Now, listen Watson," he says grimly. "This is a murder case, obviously. And I want you to find the murderer. I can't **afford** to have this sort of scandal hanging over Church Hill!"

Watson looks out to the garden and then stares at Colonel Lessons.

"But you can afford to take out £25,000 from your bank – one day before Jim Ryan is murdered. I wonder if there's a connection?"

Lessons is stunned. "Now, look here, Inspector! I don't think you realize how much my school pays in local taxes. Without this school, Eastcastle is nothing. And how do you know about the £25,000, anyway?"

"Have you got a cleaning lady, Colonel?"

Lessons sits down. What on earth is this little inspector trying to say?

"Of course we've got staff," shouts the Colonel. "Ask my daughter, Rose. She's in charge of all that."

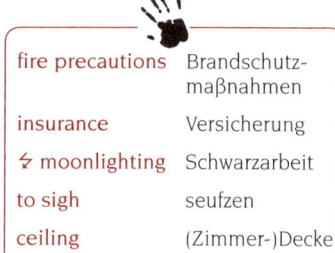

fire precautions	Brandschutz-maßnahmen
insurance	Versicherung
⚡ moonlighting	Schwarzarbeit
to sigh	seufzen
ceiling	(Zimmer-)Decke

Watson deals his trump card.

"Yes, I know. And I also know that your cleaner's name is Mrs Bradley. She comes in every weekday around six. Now, where were you, Colonel, between six and seven on Thursday? Not at the Golf Club, so they tell me."

Lessons begins to splutter. He knows exactly where he was – in his office with that bastard Jim Ryan.

"Er – wait a second, Inspector. Let's see – Thursday. Back from the clubhouse around four to check up on accounts. Last-minute preparations for Friday, you know, fire precautions, and so on. Ah, yes! A short talk with Jim Ryan about his references. He wants – sorry, he wanted to take up a post in Saudi Arabia. Well, there were no problems. He was an excellent member of staff here during his six-week stay. Then down to the Pig and Whistle for dinner. Yes, that's it. Thursday. Oh, and a phone call to Tracy to withdraw the £25,000. And, dear Inspector Watson, I need that money to pay for certain repairs to the roof, and so on. Cash payments, you know. Cash, Inspector – no tax, no insurance. I think you call it 'moonlighting'."

Inspector Watson sighs and looks at the ceiling.

"A good story, Colonel," he says. "It sounds very convincing. But Mrs Bradley tells me a very different story. She's cleaning the floor outside your office and hears a loud argument between you and Ryan. Now, she isn't an eavesdropper, but she hears a reference to the Ministry of Education and the word 'blackmail' – and the sum of £25,000. After a few minutes Ryan comes out, whistling cheerfully. Then, around seven, you come out. You are so angry that you don't even say goodbye. By the way, I also know that you have several prizes for shooting with a pistol.

eavesdropper	Lauscher(in)
cheerfully	fröhlich, heiter
constable	Wachtmeister, Polizist
reason	Grund
handcuffs *pl*	Handschellen
relieved	erleichtert
detective work	Ermittlungsarbeit
promotion	Beförderung
to gather	*hier*: (ein)sammeln
mansion	Villa, Herrenhaus
mellowed brickwork	alter Ziegelsteinbau

I'm afraid, Colonel, that I must ask you to come down to the police station."

Watson stands up and calls in the constable waiting outside. The Colonel laughs, slightly hysterically. For some reason, he sees the sun setting on Majorca and the South of France, yet again. Even on Calais.

"You've got this all wrong, Inspector. I'm totally innocent..." the Colonel splutters.

But he has no time to explain. The constable puts on the handcuffs and leads him out to the police car. The Colonel sees his gleaming Roller in the drive. This time it will be a police cell – not Number 19.

Watson is relieved. He congratulates himself. Excellent detective work, he thinks. I may get promotion for solving this case so quickly. He gathers his notes, walks to his car and then decides to have a good pint of bitter in his local pub. Church Hill School, the old Victorian mansion, is now empty. The mellowed brickwork reflects the sun as Watson slams the front door shut.

About two miles out from the harbour, Tracy, on her yacht, is gliding through the waves of the English Channel. She looks

| to admire | bewundern |
| to hum | summen |

towards the town and **admires** the old castle standing at the top of the cliffs. She doesn't feel sorry for the Colonel. He's an arrogant bastard anyway. Only Tracy knows who really killed Jim Ryan. She gently **hums** the sea shanty about Billy Boy and Nancy Grey. She thinks about the £25,000 in a brown envelope and her flight to New York on Monday. Then she suddenly turns and throws the revolver into the water.

Exercise 14: Questions. Formulieren Sie folgende Sätze als Fragen!

1. Watson is doing his interviews.

   _____

2. They order another gin.

   _____

3. He turns to the gun collection.

   _____

4. His school pays local taxes.

   _____

5. She's cleaning the floor.

   _____

6. The sun is setting on Eastcastle.

   _____

The Butterworth Mystery

Alison Romer

Scary Stories

Michael Rose had been working for the Lancashire Police for seven years. He loved his job. Because he lived and worked in a small village, he knew many people by name. Even though he was only thirty-three, he was an **old-fashioned** type of policeman: friendly, caring and ready to help. He liked the people of Pendle Lee, and the people of Pendle Lee liked Sergeant Rose.

Crime was not a big problem. At the police station, days went by quite slowly. Many other officers liked to be in a bigger town or a city. But Michael loved being part of a small **community**. The village itself was also a lovely place to live. The church, which was in the centre, had been built in 1376. Many of the houses had been standing for a very long time. Even the pub, which was called "The White **Witch**", was hundreds of years old. At the **edge** of the village a river **flowed** through the fields and woods. On summer evenings, it was as beautiful as a painting.

However, there was not very much for young people to do. Bored teenagers were often getting into trouble. In fact, most of the problems Michael had to **deal with** were caused by teenagers. Loud music, graffiti and bad behaviour were the main

old-fashioned	altmodisch
crime	Verbrechen
community	Gemeinschaft
witch	Hexe
edge	Rand, Ecke
to flow	fließen
to deal with	sich beschäftigen mit, zu tun haben mit

things. Usually he just talked to the young people and their parents. He hardly ever had to take one of them to the station. In seven years, he had only **arrested** five people. Yet in those seven years, he had found eleven lost dogs and returned them to their

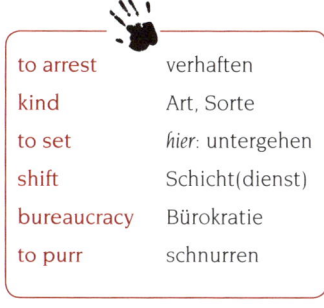

to arrest	verhaften
kind	Art, Sorte
to set	*hier*: untergehen
shift	Schicht(dienst)
bureaucracy	Bürokratie
to purr	schnurren

homes. Some policemen would have found that **kind** of life boring. But Michael was happy.

Exercise 1: Translation. Wie heißt das Wort auf Deutsch? Übersetzen Sie!

1. fields _____
2. village _____
3. caring _____
4. ancient _____
5. cottage _____
6. happen _____
7. gate _____
8. painting _____

It was the middle of summer. The sun had just **set**, and it was very late. Michael was at the police station. He was on the night **shift**. For a few hours, he had been doing some paperwork. Even in a small village station, there was a lot of **bureaucracy**. He had also had some coffee and had read the newspaper. The police station cat, Harriet, was sitting on his knee. She was **purring**.

49

"Sorry, Harriet," Michael said. "You're going to have to move. I want another coffee."

He tried to push the fat **tabby** cat off his lap, but she didn't want to go.

Suddenly the phone rang.

That's **strange**, Michael thought. Nobody ever called late at night unless something was really wrong.

He picked up the phone.

"Pendle Lee Police Station," he said.

tabby	getigerte Katze
strange	seltsam
to recognize	erkennen
elderly	älter
cemetery	Friedhof
to sigh	seufzen
to gather	*hier*: (sich) versammeln
to upset sb.	jmd. ärgern
graveyard	Friedhof
grave	Grab
right away	sofort
glow	Leuchten

"Oh, Michael," said a voice he **recognized**.

It was Mrs White, an **elderly** lady who lived on the edge of the village.

"I'm sorry it's so late," she said. "But there's something happening in the **cemetery**."

Michael **sighed**. Every now and again, a group of teenagers would **gather** at the Pendle Lee Cemetery. Wearing black clothes, they would light candles and play loud music.

"Is it those kids again?" Michael asked.

"Maybe," Mrs White replied. "I can't sleep. And it **upsets me** that they go to the **graveyard**. My parents' and grandparents' **graves** are there."

"Of course," said Michael. "I'll go **right away**. Then maybe you can get some sleep."

Around ten minutes later, Michael parked the police car at the cemetery gates. He could hear music. The yellow **glow** of candles told him where the kids were. He got out of the car and switched on his torch. Next to the gates was a very old house. In the past, the cemetery care-taker had lived in it. But the

to switch on	anschalten
torch	Taschenlampe
caretaker	Hausmeister

place had been standing empty for twenty years. Some of the windows were broken. Climbing plants had grown over the building. They had even gone through some of the windows.

Two hundred years ago, it had been really pretty. But now it looked like something from a scary movie. Nobody went inside. Birds had made their homes in the empty rooms.

Exercise 2: Choose the correct alternative.
Kreuzen Sie die richtige Variante an!

1. The graveyard at night...

    a) ☐ looked how something from a scary movie.

    b) ☐ looked like something from a scary movie.

    c) ☐ looked as something from a scary movie.

2. Police work involves...

    a) ☐ much bureaucracies.

    b) ☐ more bureaucracy.

    c) ☐ a lot of bureaucracy.

3. He knew many people by name.

    a) ☐ He called people names.

    b) ☐ He knew lots of people quite well.

    c) ☐ Many people knew his name.

Using his torch to light the way, Michael went towards the teenagers. Candles were glowing on the graves. There was loud music, and some of the teenagers were standing in a circle singing.

When Michael appeared out of the darkness, he frightened some of them. A girl screamed. "Sorry," he said to her. "It's only me. Are you trying to make a ghost appear?"

"It's none of your business," said a tall boy.

to glow	leuchten
to appear	auftauchen, erscheinen
to frighten sb.	jmd. erschrecken
to scream	schreien, kreischen
ghost	Gespenst
It's none of your business!	Das geht dich nichts an!
brave	mutig
fright	Schreck
Lancashire	engl. Grafschaft, benannt nach der Stadt Lancaster

He stepped forward into the torchlight. Michael knew who he was. His name was Alex. He was seventeen years old, and his parents owned the bakery.

"It IS my business," Michael replied. "This is a cemetery. Having a party here isn't respectful."

The girl who had nearly screamed came across to Michael.

"We can do what we want," she said. She was trying to sound brave after her fright earlier.

Michael recognized her now. Katie Lewis. She was only fourteen, and she should have been at home in bed.

"What are you doing?" Michael asked. "Are you trying to make contact with witches? I don't think you'll have any luck tonight."

Pendle Lee was in a part of Lancashire that was famous for its witches. In the early seventeenth century, some women and men from the area had been arrested. It was said that one talked to a black dog that was really the devil. The villagers believed that witches had made some people sick and even killed them. It was believed that cows stopped giving milk because of magic spells. The unlucky women and men were kept in prison at Lancaster Castle. The witches had been hung in 1612. Many people went to watch. Now, the witches were seen as ordinary people who were scapegoats of the community. But the stories had continued until the present day.

to believe	glauben
magic spell	Zauberspruch
prison	Gefängnis
to hang sb.	jmd. erhängen
scapegoat	Sündenbock
to exist	bestehen, existieren

Exercise 3: Simple past. Lesen Sie weiter und setzen Sie die Verben ins Simple Past!

The Lancashire Witches **1.** bring _____ many tourists to the area. People could buy toy witches. Lancaster Castle even **2.** have _____ a special tour of the old prison rooms. And every year on Halloween, people from all over **3.** walk _____ up Pendle Hill in the dark. Pendle Lee had its own stories, too. Some were about the cemetery. The first graves **4.** be _____ over seven hundred years old. Long before the big Pendle Lee church was built, an even older church **existed** where the cemetery **5.** be _____. The stories **6.** tell _____ of witches meeting at the place where the old church once **7.** stand _____.

It was said that they danced around large fires and tried to see the devil. The ghost of a witch called Agnes Cott was said to **haunt** the graveyard. Some people said that the caretaker's house was haunted, too. Strange noises were heard late at night. Strange lights were seen, too, even when the teenagers were in their beds.

Michael switched on his torch again.

"Time to go," he said to the kids, "before the ghost of Agnes Cott really does appear. Then you'll all run screaming back home anyway."

"You can't stop us," said Alex. "We'll come back again. The more this community hates us the happier we are."

"I'm sorry you feel that way," said Michael.

He did understand. There was nothing for teenagers to do in Pendle Lee. He thought that young people's discos at the **church hall** were a good idea. The villagers were worried about noise and alcohol. However, having teenagers on the streets at night was a bigger problem.

to haunt	spuken (in)
church hall	Gemeindesaal
headstone	Grabstein
to smash	zerschlagen, zerschmettern

After the kids left the graveyard, Michael looked around. There wasn't any graffiti on the graves tonight. In the past, there had been a problem with graffiti. Even some of the **headstones** had been **smashed**. That was a few years ago.

Alex and the other young people were angry and bored, but Michael didn't think they would do anything that bad. He decided to keep an eye on them anyway.

A few days later, Michael was on a normal afternoon shift. He liked to work during the day because there was more to do. He could walk around the village and talk to people. He could stop by the different shops and chat with the owners. At the station, other officers would come in from time to time. Even Harriet the cat liked the daytime best. On sunny days, she could lie on the step outside the station. Anybody coming in or going out would have to step over her.

Mr Murphy, an elderly man, had called in at the station to give

to stop by	vorbeischauen
to chat	plaudern
allotment	Schrebergarten
rather	*hier*: eher
to admire	bewundern
mobile	Handy
emergency	Notfall
to burgle sth.	einbrechen in
siren	Sirene
art resto-ration	Gemälde-restaurierung
to offer	(an)bieten
to think long and hard	es sich reiflich überlegen

Michael some beans. Mr Murphy had grown them himself in his allotment. He was always stopping by with fresh vegetables. Like many older people, he used his allotment for pleasure rather than needing the food. He grew more than he could eat. Michael was just admiring the fresh green beans when his mobile rang.

"I'll just get that," Michael said to Mr Murphy.

He put the beans down. The call was from his boss, who had an office in the city.

"We've just heard from the Oswald Gallery," the Chief Inspector said. "They called the national emergency number. Can you go there, Michael? They've been burgled."

Michael switched on the sirens as he drove quickly through the village in his car. As he drove, he thought about the gallery. He hadn't been there for over three years, but he used to go a lot. That was because his ex-girlfriend, Sarah, loved art. Sarah had left to go to America about three years ago. She worked in art restoration and had been offered a job in Boston. After thinking long and hard, she decided to take it. But Michael couldn't get a job with the police in the United States. He didn't want to stop being a policeman either. So he stayed in Pendle Lee, and Sarah moved to Boston.

The Oswald Gallery was just outside the village. It was in a beautiful eighteenth-century house. A man called John Oswald had built the house, and the gallery was named after him. It took Michael around ten minutes to get there. When he arrived, he walked to the door. Two elderly women quickly came to meet him. They looked upset. Both of them started speaking at once. "Oh Sergeant,[i] thank goodness you're here!" one of the women exclaimed. "I'm Joan Potts. I work here."

"We don't know how it happened," the other lady was saying

> Nur als direkte Anrede oder als Teil eines Namens werden Titel und Berufsbezeichnungen wie **Sergeant** im Englischen großgeschrieben. In allen anderen Fällen schreibt man sie klein.

at the same time, "but it's my fault!"

"No, Lottie, of course it's not your fault," said Joan.

"Yes it is!" Lottie exclaimed. "I'm so angry with myself!"

Michael raised his hands.

"Let's stay calm," he said. "We'll go inside, and you can tell me all about it. Then we'll start searching for the thief."

upset	erschrocken, aufgebracht
at once	*hier*: gleichzeitig
Thank goodness!	Gott sei Dank!
to exclaim	ausrufen
fault	Fehler
thief	Dieb

Past Life

Once inside, Michael took out his notebook.

"Now tell me what happened," he said.

"No one had come to visit for over two hours," said Joan Potts. "It was a slow day."

Lottie Bingley sat down behind the reception desk.

"I'm afraid I left the reception," she said. "Every year we have a competition for artists. People from all over Lancashire send in their paintings. This morning we

reception	Empfang
competition	Wettbewerb
to unpack	auspacken
to steal	stehlen
security camera	Überwachungskamera

had some new paintings come in, and I was very excited. I wanted to see them, even though it's not my job to unpack them. I went upstairs to look. While I was gone, someone came in and stole one of our paintings. So it's all my fault."

Michael looked all around the room.

"Don't you have security cameras?" he asked.

"No," Joan replied. "It would cost a lot of money. But we never imagined that someone would steal from the Oswald Gallery!"

"And neither of you saw anybody?" Michael asked.

"No." Both women replied at the same time.

"We didn't see or hear anything," said Lottie.

"Let's have a look at where the painting was hung," Michael said. The women led him into one of the gallery's little rooms. Modern galleries had lots of space and white paint, but the Oswald Gallery was different. The building had many small rooms and **halls**. The walls were covered in beautiful old wood. The windows were very small. As visitors walked around, they could imagine living three hundred years ago. Paintings were hung on all the walls, but in one place there was an empty spot.

"It was here," said Joan. "It was called 'Summer'."

Michael took out his phone.

"I'm going to call the **crime scene** police," he told Joan and Lottie. "Someone will come round and check for **fingerprints**. I'll also need a photograph of the painting, please. It'll help in the **investigation**."

hall	Flur
crime scene	Tatort
fingerprint	Fingerabdruck
investigation	Ermittlung

"I'll go and find one," said Lottie. "The artist was Butterworth, of course."

The Oswald Gallery was small and not very important. But it had the largest collection of Butterworth paintings in the country. Tristan Butterworth was a famous painter from the 1940s and 50s. He had lived near Pendle Lee for many years. When he died in the 1980s, many of his best paintings were given to the gallery. People came from all over the United Kingdom to see them.

Lottie came back into the reception and handed a large photograph to Michael.

"Here it is," she said. "This is 'Summer'. It's a wonderful picture, isn't it?"

Michael looked at it. It showed a beautiful summer scene. In the background, the sun shone on a river. Green fields and trees were all around. In the front of the painting, there was a large tree, and under it sat a young woman. She was wearing an old-fashioned yellow dress and a big hat.

"This was painted in 1951," Lottie said. "Looking at it makes me feel so calm. It almost feels like you're really there."

"It's lovely," said Michael. "I'll need to keep this photograph for our investigation. Is that okay?"

"Of course," said Lottie. "We'll do whatever we can to help."

Exercise 5: Question words. Setzen Sie die richtigen Fragepronomen ein!

which   who   where   why   what   when

1. _____ was the painting hung?

2. _____ kind of competition was it?

3. _____ does the gallery open?

4. _____ of the paintings was stolen?

5. _____ were Joan and Lottie so upset?

6. _____ works at the gallery?

Back inside his car, Michael phoned his boss, Chief Inspector Blake. He gave Blake all the information he had so far. The inspector was very busy. Michael could tell he wasn't very interested in a painting stolen from a village gallery. The city had more crime than the police could deal with.

"They should have had security cameras," Blake said angrily.

He told Michael to contact the Art Loss Register. It kept an international **database** of art that had

| database | Datenbank |

been stolen or lost. If a rich person or a museum wanted to buy a piece of art, they could find out if it was stolen through the Register. If it was, the buyer could **alert** the police. The thief who was trying to sell the art could then be caught.

to alert sb.	jmd. alarmieren, warnen
burglary	Einbruch (-diebstahl)
mood	Stimmung, Laune
terror alert	Terroralarm
wavy	gewellt
to wonder	sich fragen
imagination	Vorstellung

It was hard to find stolen art. Sometimes the buyer knew it was stolen, but didn't care. Sometimes a group of thieves would plan a big **burglary**, and then wait for many years before selling the art in places like Africa or South America.

"Can you deal with this?" Blake asked Michael. "I don't have another officer who can come down there right now. It's too bad we have to send you a crime scene officer just to take some fingerprints."

"I still think it's a good idea," Michael said.

The inspector was often in a bad **mood**, and Michael was glad he didn't have to work in the city with him.

"You know we're on **terror alert**, don't you?" Blake went on. "We may have to send officers to Manchester or London at any moment. You too, Sergeant."

"I know," Michael replied. "Leave everything to me, Inspector. I'll send you my reports."

After the phone call was finished, Michael opened the car window. He took a deep breath of fresh air. Then he looked at the photograph of 'Summer' again. The young woman in the picture was very pretty. She had long, **wavy** blonde hair. She looked out across the fields. Michael **wondered** if the woman had been real or if she had come from the painter's **imagination**.

Michael was soon back at the station. He immediately contacted the Art Loss Register. He informed them about the stolen painting and gave all the details. Then he went out and interviewed the villagers. He was hoping someone had seen something strange, like someone hurrying away from the village. Meanwhile, the crime scene officer was exploring the

to interview	befragen, verhören
meanwhile	währenddessen
to explore	erkunden
to match with	*hier*: passen zu
Crimestoppers number	Telefonnummer für sachdienliche Hinweise
stranger	Fremder
unconscious	bewusstlos
straight	direkt, geradewegs

gallery. If fingerprints were found, they would be put into the police fingerprint database. If the thief had done anything wrong before, his (or her) prints would be in the database. They would match with the prints from the crime scene. Then the police would have a name.

Over the next two days, Michael was busy. He put up signs about the burglary. The signs asked people with any information to call the police or the national Crimestoppers number. He also went from house to house, asking the villagers if they had seen a stranger in the village. A few couples and families had had picnics or had stopped at the White Witch pub. But nobody had been behaving strangely. He made copies of the 'Summer' photograph. Then he took them to all the art shops and auction houses in the area. He sent the photo to colleagues in Preston, Manchester, and even London.

At the station, he put the photo on the wall. Instead of trying to find a stolen painting, he began to feel that he was trying to find the beautiful woman. It seemed very important to take her back to the gallery where she lived.

Exercise 6: Prepositions. Lesen Sie weiter und setzen Sie die passenden Präpositionen ein!

in   about   for   with   at   to   after

1. _____ a few days, the other police officers started to joke **2.** _____ Michael's painting. He looked **3.** _____ it a hundred times a day. Sometimes, when he was talking **4.** _____ someone, his eyes would go to the photograph. "Have you fallen **5.** _____ love?" some of the officers asked.

Michael no longer chatted **6.** _____ the villagers. He didn't seem to have time any more. Even Harriet the cat seemed in a bad mood because of 'Summer'. Michael only wanted to hunt **7.** _____ the painting, and was no longer interested in playing with her.

Whenever he had a moment, he was on the phone or visiting auction houses, asking about the painting. Even when he was not at work, he'd visit places that sold old paintings.

On Tuesday afternoon, the phone rang. It was exactly five days since 'Summer' had been stolen. Every time the phone rang, Michael hoped it was about the painting. It was Joan Potts from the gallery.

"Something terrible has happened!" she exclaimed. "Lottie has been taken to hospital. Another painting was stolen and this time, the thief pushed Lottie down the stairs. She's unconscious."

After going straight to the gallery and looking at the crime scene, Michael went to the hospital with Joan. They were both very worried about Lottie. Because she was old, her chances of getting better quickly were not good. She'd hit her head quite **badly** and broken one of her legs.

Joan couldn't help crying as they stood in the waiting room

badly	*hier*: heftig, schwer
in charge	verantwortlich, zuständig
landscape	Landschaft
still-life	Stillleben
clue	Hinweis, Spur

at the hospital. The doctor **in charge** promised to call Michael as soon as there was a change. Michael needed to ask her about what happened. Perhaps Lottie saw the thief coming up the stairs. But while she was unconscious and in danger, all he could do was wait and hope.

Meanwhile, he needed to contact the Art Loss Register about the second stolen painting. It was another Butterworth, called 'Evening in June'. This time it was of a terrace outside a lovely old house. There was a table with teacups and a teapot, and a large strawberry cake. On one of the chairs sat a woman. Michael recognized her as the woman from 'Summer'. This time she was dressed in a pretty purple dress. She was reading a book. In the background were green hills, and the sun was just going down. The sunset seemed to make the picture glow.

Michael thought it was strange that both paintings were of the same woman. There were many Butterworth pictures that showed **landscapes** or **still-life** scenes. Only a few had the young woman in them. Perhaps that was a **clue**.

"Who was she?" Michael asked when he called Joan that night.

"Don't you know?" asked Joan. "It's Sylvia. Sylvia and Tristan Butterworth got married in 1950. She was very beautiful and was his model for some of his paintings."

"Maybe if we find out more about Sylvia Butterworth, it might give us a clue," Michael said. "Perhaps the thief wants to collect paintings of her."

"Good idea," said Joan. "Maybe he's obsessed with her. We have an archive at the gallery. It has a lot of information about Sylvia in it. You can look at it if you like."

Exercise 7: Opposites. Finden Sie das passende Gegenteil!

1. ☐ few
2. ☐ push
3. ☐ wrong
4. ☐ friendly
5. ☐ normal
6. ☐ slow
7. ☐ daytime
8. ☐ beautiful
9. ☐ loud

a) strange
b) quiet
c) pull
d) ugly
e) many
f) right
g) fast
h) unfriendly
i) night-time

The next day, after his afternoon shift, Michael went back to the Oswald Gallery. It had been closed, and there were plans to buy security cameras. The risk of someone getting hurt again was too big. Joan took Michael upstairs to a small office. It was filled with filing cabinets.

"This is the Butterworth archive," Joan said. "The filing cabinets are full of photographs and letters. They belonged to both Tristan

obsessed (with)	besessen (von)
archive	Archiv
to hurt	verletzen; schmerzen
filing cabinet	Aktenschrank

and Sylvia. There are also lots of papers about Butterworth's paintings and exhibitions. You can look through them, if you like."

Joan made him a cup of coffee. Then she gave him the keys to the gallery and the code number of the alarm system. She went back to the hospital, where she spent her evenings sitting with Lottie. Michael was alone. He didn't know where to start looking. All he knew was that someone had a reason for stealing Butterworth's paintings of Sylvia. Perhaps the past would give him a clue.

exhibition	Ausstellung
reason	Grund
file	Akte
confident	selbstsicher
down	*hier*: offen, lose
gorgeous	herrlich, wunderschön
honeymoon	Flitterwochen

First he pulled open some files of photographs. There were lots of black-and-white ones, and there were many of Sylvia by herself. Michael knew they were not important for the investigation, but he couldn't help looking. Some were of Sylvia when she was very young. Most showed her in her twenties and thirties.

Michael felt that he had never seen anyone more beautiful. Sylvia had big, dark eyes and a glowing smile. She was quite tall and looked strong and confident. When she was younger, she had worn her long hair down. When she was older, she wore it up, in the style of the 1950s. Her clothes were always pretty and looked good on her. In some of the photos, she was with a man. Michael recognized him as Tristan Butterworth. The names, places and dates were written on the backs of many photos.

There were many pictures, for example, of Tristan and Sylvia in a gorgeous landscape. In the background were lakes and mountains. On the backs of the pictures were the words 'Honeymoon, Cumbria, 1950'. The couple looked very happy. Some of the photographs showed other people, too.

There were many that had been taken on the terrace of a house. Michael thought it was the same terrace as in 'Evening in June'. In the photos, lots

| soldier | Soldat |
| serious | ernst |

of people were standing around. They had glasses of wine and cigarettes. In other photos, the same people were sitting under a tree, having a picnic. Behind them the Pendle Lee river flowed. Everyone was smiling at the camera. There were a few pictures of Butterworth with another man. The pictures said 'Nigel and Tristan', with different places and dates. There were also pictures of 'Nigel and Sylvia'.

Next he looked at some old letters. There were lots from Sylvia to Tristan. Michael began to read. He read for a long time. When he looked at his watch, he had been reading for over an hour. He had been in a different world. It seemed as though Sylvia was writing to him. He put down the letters and picked up some different ones. All of them were to Sylvia from a man named Nigel Huxley. Some were dated from 1941 to 1944 and had been sent from France.

Exercise 8: Adjectives or adverbs? Lesen Sie weiter und wählen Sie das passende Adjektiv oder Adverb!

Michael looked through them **1.** quick / quickly . Huxley had written about being a soldier in World War II. He wrote about being frightened when bombs fell **2.** close / closely by. He also told her about other soldiers, who had died. Some of the letters were very **3.** serious / seriously .

But others were **4.** full / fully of fun. In these light letters, he wrote about parties and friends. Huxley had written 'To my darling Sylvia' at the top of the letters. It was **5.** clear / clearly that he had been in love with her. Michael took out his notebook and wrote down Nigel's name. Perhaps he was still **6.** alive / alively . Maybe he had more information about Sylvia and the paintings.

Michael had been in the archive for hours. At last he decided to go home. He wanted to come back as soon as possible, because there were many more letters and papers to look at. But before he left, Michael opened the filing cabinet with the photos. There was one he wanted to see again. The photo showed Sylvia sitting on a beach. She was wearing a big sun hat and a white dress. Her hair was down. In her hands was a small book. She had stopped reading and was looking into the camera. But instead of smiling, Sylvia looked serious. Michael felt that she was looking right at him. Before he could stop himself, he had picked up the photo. Then he put it into his pocket. He had never stolen anything in his life. Now he was a thief, just like the person who had taken the paintings.

Michael had spent many hours in the archive, and it was now night-time. On his way home, he drove past the cemetery. He was worried that the teenagers were there again. Suddenly, he saw something. It looked like the glow from a candle or a torch. It seemed to be moving among the graves.
"Those kids!" Michael said out loud.

He looked at his watch: 12:16 a.m. Michael stopped the car at the gates and got out his torch. Then he went into the cemetery. The light seemed to have **disappeared**. He listened, but he couldn't hear anything. The

among	zwischen
to disappear	verschwinden
to hide	(sich) verstecken
to be about to do sth.	im Begriff sein, etw. zu tun

moon was shining brightly, and the air smelled like cut grass and old flowers. He walked on. The graves looked quite scary in the dark. Although he didn't believe in ghosts, Michael didn't feel very brave. It was like a graveyard scene from a scary movie.

Suddenly he got angry. The teenagers were probably **hiding** from him. Maybe Alex and his friends were all sitting behind the headstones, waiting for him to go away. They probably thought this was funny. Michael decided to switch off his torch[1] and wait for the kids to come out.

The moonlight helped him to see quite well. But suddenly a cloud moved across the sky, and the moonlight disappeared. It was very dark. Michael turned around in a circle. Nothing. No light. And he still couldn't hear anything, either

He **was about to** switch his torch back on when he saw a small light. It was near the old caretaker's house. There was someone there. Michael put on his torch again.

Bei vielen **Phrasal Verbs** kann das Objekt sowohl vor als auch nach der Präposition stehen:
He switched his torch off.
Ein Objektpronomen steht aber immer vor der Präposition:
He switched it off.

He shone it across the graves towards the empty old house.
"Hello!" he called out.

Immediately the candlelight disappeared. Michael started to walk to the house.

"It's Sergeant Rose here," he shouted. "What are you doing?"

1. paint   cook   photograph   draw
2. moonlight   torchlight   sunlight   starlight
3. ghost   witch   vampire   murderer
4. steal   rob   burgle   sell
5. box   circle   triangle   square
6. graveyard   museum   headstone   cemetery
7. torch   candle   soldier   lamp
8. clue   confident   obsessed   frightened

When he reached the house, he shone his torch all around. There was nobody there. However, a strange symbol had appeared on the front door. It showed three stars inside a circle, painted in yellow paint. He tried the door, but it wouldn't open. He went up to some of the windows and shone his torch inside. The rooms were empty apart from some

| apart from | außer |
| spider's web | Spinnennetz |

broken tables and chairs. There were spider's webs everywhere. "Whoever you are," Michael said to the empty air, "you should go home."

Suddenly he heard a ghostly laugh. He couldn't tell if it was a man's or a woman's voice. Before he could turn around, there was a sharp pain in his head, and he was falling towards the ground.

3 Young Woman with Flowers

When Michael finally opened his eyes, his clothes were wet from lying in the grass for a long time. He put his hand to his head. When he looked at his hand, there was something dark on his fingers. Blood. He felt sick, and his head hurt. His torch was lying on the ground, but it wasn't working any more. Michael looked around. He didn't know what to do. The best thing would be to call his boss, then go to the hospital and get a doctor to look at him. He stood up. All he wanted to do was get into bed. Slowly, he went back to his car and drove home.

| witness | Zeuge |

Early the next morning, Michael went to the station. He wrote a report about what happened in the graveyard. His head still hurt badly, but he didn't want to spend the day waiting to see a doctor. Instead he called the hospital about Lottie. She was still unconscious, and the doctors were doing all sorts of tests. After the hospital call, he phoned the homes of Alex and some of the other teenagers from the cemetery. He asked their parents to bring them down to the station as soon as possible. If Alex had hit Michael, he was in serious trouble. Then he arranged for another officer to talk to the teenagers. Although Michael wanted to talk to Alex and the others himself, he was a witness

> Verwechseln Sie nicht **if** und **when:**
> *If Alex hit Michael, he would be in trouble.* (**if** = wenn, falls)
> ***When** Alex hit Michael, he was in trouble.* (**when** = wenn, als)

71

to a crime. He couldn't be the questioning officer, too. Then Michael searched the Internet for Nigel Huxley. Huxley might have information about the paintings or Sylvia. He found

sculptor	Bildhauer
nearby	in der Nähe
to pay sb. a visit	jmd. einen Besuch abstatten
mansion	Villa, Herrenhaus

out that Huxley had also been an artist. He was a sculptor, but he was not as famous as Butterworth. His last sculpture was made in 1967. Now Huxley lived in a village only 20 kilometres from Pendle Lee. He was 85 years old, and it seemed that he was very rich.

Michael thought about everything he now knew about Huxley. He lived nearby and knew about art. And although he was old, you didn't have to be fit to push an old lady downstairs. He had been in love with Sylvia. Perhaps he had driven to the gallery. He could have stolen 'Summer' while Lottie was looking at the new paintings upstairs. The second time, Lottie may have seen him stealing 'Evening in June'. He might have pushed her down the stairs, then put the painting in the car and driven home.

Michael decided to pay Huxley a visit.

But first, he put out some cat food for Harriet. The big tabby was still in a bad mood. Michael just wanted to talk about, think about and dream about those paintings! He had no time for cats or the other villagers. When Mr Murphy came in that morning with a bag of aubergines, Michael had simply thanked him and looked back at the computer.

At lunch time, Michael drove to the nearby village. It took him a long time to find Huxley's house. The house was very large. In fact, it was a mansion, but it was hidden behind lots of trees on the edge of the village. Michael parked the police car in front of the house. It was a lovely old place. There were lots of steps leading to a big door. Michael went up and rang the bell. After a few moments, an elderly woman opened the door.

"Mrs Huxley?" Michael asked.

"No, I'm the **housekeeper**," the woman said.

She looked at his police uniform and car. For some reason, she didn't seem too happy.

"Do you want to see Mr Huxley?"

"Yes, please, if he's at home," Michael replied.

"You'd better come in," said the housekeeper.

Michael followed her into the house.

| housekeeper | Haushälterin |
| to point to | zeigen auf |

"Wait here." The housekeeper **pointed to** a chair by the door.

She wasn't friendly at all. Michael wondered if she ever smiled. He sat down. The big hall was painted a light green. The floor was made of gorgeous dark wood. In the corner stood a large sculpture. Michael couldn't really tell what it was. It could have been a woman with long wavy hair. Or a tree. Whatever it was, it looked very modern.

Suddenly the housekeeper appeared again.

"You can see Mr Huxley now," she said. "He's in the living room."

Nigel Huxley sat in a big chair. He didn't look 85 at all. He seemed a lot younger. But perhaps that was because of his bright blue eyes. He looked intelligent and full of energy.

"I'm sorry about my housekeeper," Huxley said. "She's not very nice to visitors, even policemen."

Michael looked around the living room. The sun was shining through the large windows. There were two huge sofas and a few chairs. In the middle of the room was a round table. Lots of books were everywhere: on the table, on bookshelves and

| bright | *hier*: hell, strahlend |
| fireplace | (offener) Kamin |

on the floor. There was also a beautiful old fireplace. Above the fireplace, on the wall, there was a painting. Michael immediately recognized Sylvia.

"That's a Butterworth picture!" he exclaimed.

"Yes," Huxley said. "It's called 'Young Woman with Flowers'. Tristan Butterworth gave it to me."

The painting showed Sylvia holding lots of flowers. They were pink, orange and red. The background was a dark green, and Sylvia was wearing a green dress.

Michael couldn't take his eyes off the picture. Even when the housekeeper came in with tea and biscuits, he couldn't stop looking at Sylvia.

"How can I help you?" Huxley asked, taking a cup of tea and a chocolate biscuit.

Michael finally took his eyes off the painting and looked at the old man.

"I'm sorry, Mr Huxley, I should have introduced myself. I'm Sergeant Rose from the police station at Pendle Lee. You heard about the robbery at the gallery?" asked Michael.

"Of course," Huxley replied. "I collect Butterworth paintings. I'm often at the Oswald Gallery."

robbery	Raubüberfall
to question sb.	jdn. befragen
detective work	Ermittlungsarbeit

"You know that Lottie Bingley is unconscious in hospital?" Michael asked, watching Huxley closely.

"Yes. It's very sad and upsetting," Huxley said.

Michael looked at the picture of Sylvia above the fireplace.

"Somebody wanted those pictures very badly," he said. "Badly enough to almost kill an elderly woman. Both paintings were of Sylvia. We should look for someone who is obsessed with her."

Huxley's eyes shone, and he gave a small smile.

"So you've come to question me," he said. "Good detective work, Sergeant Rose. It's true, I was in love with Sylvia. She and I grew up together. Our families were friends. We lived in the same village and went to the same church. Even when I was a teenager, I loved her. I met Tristan Butterworth at art school. Sylvia would model for us both. Then the Second World War started. I became a soldier, but Tristan couldn't join the army. He had polio when he was a baby, and there was something wrong with his leg. While I was in France, Tristan and Sylvia fell in love. I wanted them to be happy, so we stayed friends."

Ein falscher Freund!
to become heißt „werden".

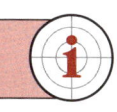

"What happened to Tristan and Sylvia?" Michael asked. He'd almost forgotten about the stolen art.

Exercise 11: Choose the correct alternative. Lesen Sie weiter und unterstreichen Sie die richtige Variante!

"The Butterworths moved to America in the 1960s," Huxley 1. goes / went on. "We 2. have written / wrote letters at Christmas, but after a few years our letters stopped. I 3. hear / heard they 4. lived / were living in New York. Tristan had an exhibition at the Museum of Modern Art. Then I read in the paper that he had died in 1986. I never saw Sylvia again. I tried 5. to find / finding her, but with no luck. Now my paintings 6. of / from Sylvia 7. bring / brought back wonderful memories of summer."

"Would you break the law to get more of those memories?" Michael asked.

"I'm sorry to disappoint you," said Huxley, "but I didn't steal those paintings."

"So you won't mind if I have a look around your house?" Michael asked.

memory	Erinnerung
to break the law	das Gesetz brechen
to disappoint sb.	jmd. enttäuschen
to mind sth.	etw. dagegen haben
search warrant	Durchsuchungs-befehl

"Yes, I do mind, Sergeant Rose," the old man replied, standing up. "My house is private. If you don't have a search warrant, please leave."

Huxley was starting to get angry. But Michael knew he was right. Without a search warrant, the police couldn't search someone's home. Michael had to leave. He thanked Huxley for his time.

On his way out to the car again, he thought about the old man. Firstly, he seemed obsessed with Sylvia and collected paintings of her. Secondly, he was **familiar with** the Oswald Gallery and lived close by. Thirdly, he didn't want the police looking around his house.

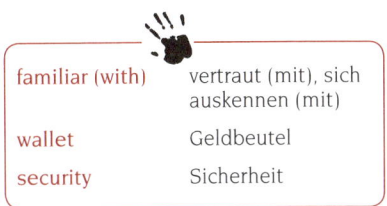

familiar (with)	vertraut (mit), sich auskennen (mit)
wallet	Geldbeutel
security	Sicherheit

Michael decided to call Chief Inspector Blake to find out if he could get a search warrant for the mansion.

Later that night, Michael decided to go to the gallery. He wanted to look in the archives again, and still had the key. He wasn't really thinking about the investigation. He was wondering if Sylvia was still alive in New York or somewhere else. She would be an old woman by now. In his imagination, however, she was a beautiful young woman. He wanted her to stay that way. He still kept the photo of Sylvia in his **wallet**. Every now and then, he took it out and looked at it.

Before he left for the gallery, he called Joan Potts. He wanted to let her know that he would visit the archive.

Now that the gallery was closed, she believed the paintings would be safe. However, she was still happy to know that a policeman was around. She also told him that they had bought a new **security** system. There were cameras for every room. In two days' time[i] it would be installed. Then

> Statt in **two days' time** kann man auch einfach **in two days** sagen. Beides bedeutet „in zwei Tagen". Die Wendung in ... days' time hebt aber die Zeitspanne, die vergeht, etwas mehr hervor.

they could open the gallery again. Meanwhile, Lottie was out of danger. She could open her eyes and talk a little bit. She had no memories at all of the robbery. She was **confused** about being in the hospital. Still, Michael was **relieved** that she was getting better.

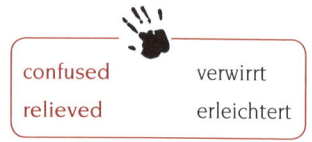

| confused | verwirrt |
| relieved | erleichtert |

Exercise 12: True or false? Kreuzen Sie die richtigen Aussagen an!

1. Nigel Huxley is 75 years old. ❏

2. Huxley had been in love with Sylvia. ❏

3. Michael thinks that Huxley might have pushed Lottie down the stairs. ❏

4. Huxley allows Michael to search his house. ❏

5. After the Second World War, Huxley lost contact to Sylvia and Tristan Butterworth. ❏

6. Michael kept a photo of Sylvia in his wallet. ❏

4 Voices in the Dark

By the time Michael got to the Oswald Gallery, the sun had nearly disappeared. He parked his car right in front of the door and was shocked about what he saw. There was graffiti all over the front of the building. It was the same yellow paint that he'd seen at the caretaker's house, and the same symbols. Then he saw the broken window. The hole was big enough for someone to climb through, but bits of glass were still sharp.

The robber had probably been hurt. Michael looked through the broken window. A big rock from the garden was lying inside, on the wooden floor. Bits of broken glass were everywhere. On one piece of glass, he saw something red. It looked like blood. The thief had been cut. This meant that the police could get an important DNA clue. Michael immediately took out his mobile phone. He called the city station. Another officer would come to Pendle Lee as soon as possible. The crime scene officer would come, too.

Michael didn't want to stand outside waiting. He decided to go in. Perhaps the thief was still in the gallery. Trying to stay calm, he opened the front door. Then he stopped and listened. He couldn't hear anything. He took another step. The wooden floor made a loud noise. Then, slowly and quietly, he went to the room with the broken window. There were paintings on the wall. Some of them were landscapes from the Butterworth collection. There were also sculptures. But Michael was more interested in the blood. It was a very dark red because it was almost dry. It made a small trail across the floor and into the hall. Michael followed it. The trail went up the stairs, along the hall, and into another room. It stopped in front of a wall. There was an empty space where a painting once hung.

Suddenly, there was a shout from downstairs. The two other policemen had arrived. Michael went downstairs and greeted them. He told them about the trail of blood and the stolen painting.

"Can you go through the building?" he asked the constable, whose name was John Ritchie. "I'm going to look in the garden."

"I'll get fingerprints and blood," said the crime scene officer. "But I don't think we'll get a match. There were no matches on our fingerprint database last time."

Just as Michael was about to go outside, the constable called him back.

"You're the one who was hit in the graveyard, aren't you?" he asked. "I talked to those teenagers. Every single one has an alibi. Even Alex, who is an angry young man. One day he'll end up arrested for something, believe me!"

Michael thanked him, then took his torch and went outside.

trail	Spur
to greet sb.	jmd. grüßen
constable	Wachtmeister, Polizist
match	*hier*: Treffer

There was no moonlight, so it was very dark. He walked all around the building, looking and listening. On one side of the garden was the car park. Two police cars were parked there. On the other side of the garden there were woods. They made a good hiding place. Michael went into the trees. It was very dark, almost black. The trees looked very tall in the white light from the torch. Michael thought about his visits to the cemetery. Now he was walking through woods at night. His torch had become his best friend. It was a good thing he did not believe in ghosts or witches. If they were real, he would have seen one by now. In fact, he felt like the ghost of Pendle Lee himself. That's what happened when you spent too much time in graveyards and dark places.

Exercise 13: Personal pronouns. Ersetzen Sie die hervorgehobenen Personen durch die richtigen Pronomen!

1. **Lottie** *She* was pushed down the stairs.
2. **Two policemen**   were helping with the investigation.
3. **You and I**   don't know who the thief is.
4. **Michael**   followed the trail of blood upstairs.
5. Michael told **Lottie and Joan**   to get cameras.
6. Can you tell **my friend and I**   where the gallery is?
7. We will visit **Lottie**   in the hospital.
8. Tell **Michael**   about the stolen painting!
9. "I'm here to help **the woman**   ," Michael told her.
10. "Don't   have security cameras?" he asked **Lottie and Joan**.

Suddenly, he heard a noise. He immediately [i] stopped walking and listened. He wondered if it was a small animal making noises in the dark. But then he heard a voice. Another voice answered. Two people were hiding in the woods. Michael took out his phone and called PC Ritchie. He spoke very quietly and quickly. The constable agreed to join him.

> Abweichend zum Deutschen stehen **Adverbien in der Satzmitte** im Englischen nicht hinter dem konjugierten Verb, sondern davor.
> *Sergeant Rose **often** goes to the cemetery.*
> Er geht **oft** zum Friedhof.
> *He **immediately** stopped walking when he heard a noise.*
> Er blieb **sofort** stehen, als er ein Geräusch hörte.

In less than a minute, the constable was there, walking softly through the trees. Then they both switched off their torches. After a few moments, their eyes could see better in the darkness. They quietly walked towards the sound of voices. Two people were hiding in some bushes underneath a tree. They were dressed all in black, and had long black hair. This just made their white faces stand out even more in the dark. Michael recognized two young men from the ceme-

PC (Police Constable)	Wachtmeister
to manage to do sth.	es schaffen, etw. zu tun

tery. He gave a shout. The boys looked around and saw the officers, then jumped up and started to run. Michael and PC Ritchie raced after them through the trees. The teen-agers were fast, but frightened. They kept looking behind them. Suddenly, one of them hit a tree and fell to the ground.

"It's a good idea to look where you're going," said Michael as he pulled the boy to his feet.

Meanwhile, PC Ritchie had managed to stop the other one. The constable took the boy's rucksack and opened it. He shone his torch inside.

"What do we have here, boys?" PC Ritchie asked, shining his light on cans of yellow spray paint.

spray paint	Sprühfarbe
involved in	beteiligt an
insulting	beleidigend

At the police station, Michael and PC Ritchie questioned the teenagers. They said they'd painted the symbols on the walls, but had had nothing to do with the smashed window or the burglary. Just after doing the graffiti, they'd heard someone walking through the car park. They'd gone into the woods and then heard the sound of breaking glass. One of the boys' fathers was in the room with them, which was normal when a 15-year-old was involved in a crime.

"Why didn't you call the police?" he asked his son.

"I hate the pigs," said the boy, using the insulting word for policemen. "Can we go now?"

Exercise 14: Plurals. Geben Sie die Pluralform an!

1. thief _____

2. woman _____

3. gallery _____

4. information _____

5. memory _____

6. noise _____

7. system _____

8. witch _____

The police would wait until daylight to search the woods for the stolen painting. Michael didn't want to let the boys go until then, but he had to. There was no reason for arresting them. They were checked for cuts, because of the broken glass in the gallery window. But neither of the boys had been cut anywhere on their bodies.

They were in lots of trouble about the graffiti, but Michael didn't think anything serious would happen to them. He let them go home with their parents.

Back at his desk, he made some notes for his report. Then he made a list of things to do in the morning. At the top was the search warrant for Nigel Huxley's home. He wanted to visit the old sculptor as soon as possible. He wanted to have some of Huxley's blood for testing, too. The investigators could match it against the blood from the gallery. Next, he wanted to take Joan Potts to the gallery to ask her about the stolen painting. He was sure it was another one of Sylvia. Then, he wanted to go to the hospital to see if Lottie had any memories of the robbery. Suddenly, the phone rang. Michael picked it up.

"Hello?" he said.

"Michael, it's Mrs White," said the woman on the phone. "Sorry I'm calling so late. It's those kids in the cemetery."

"Not again." Michael sighed.

He was disappointed. There were bigger things than bad behaviour going on in Pendle Lee.

"I'll go immediately," he said. It wasn't illegal to be at a cemetery at night, but it wasn't respectful.

"Perhaps we can ask the ghost of Agnes Cott to give them a fright," Mrs White said. "Then they'll stay at home every night!"

Michael gave a short laugh.

"I'll ask her to pay them a visit," he said.

Once more, Michael drove to the cemetery. Once more, he parked at the gates and got out his torch. There were candles glowing among the graves. He could see young people sitting around. Loud music was playing. He recognized the tall figure of Alex. When he got close to the group, Alex saw him and stood up. The young man looked angry. Michael felt angry, too, but he didn't want to get involved in a fight with teenagers.

"Go away!" Alex yelled.

Michael was just about to reply when he heard a loud scream. It sounded like it was coming from the caretaker's cottage. Immediately Michael started to run to the old house. Alex ran, too.

"It's Katie!" Alex exclaimed. "She went into the house for a dare."

"Can't you kids stay out of trouble?" Michael shouted as he ran.

When he got to the house, he tried to open the door. It was still locked.

"She went through a window," said Alex.

Together they ran to the side of the building. Just then, Katie screamed again. Michael found the window. It was old-fashioned, and the old wood had made it easy to open from the outside. He shone his torch inside and called Katie's name. He saw her rush into the room, looking very frightened. When she saw Michael and Alex, she started to cry and immediately tried to climb through the window. Michael helped her.

Once outside, Katie fell on the ground. She lay on the grass.

"It's the witch!" she said. She couldn't stop crying.

"What did she look like?" Alex asked.

figure	*hier*: Gestalt; Figur
to yell	(laut) schreien
dare	Mutprobe
to rush	eilen, sich beeilen

Michael looked at the young man angrily. "There are no witches," he said. "Or ghosts."

Then he saw a strange glow coming from inside the house. It was very bright orange.

Katie and Alex saw it, too.

"I dropped my candle," said Katie.

The old house **was on fire**.

Michael immediately pulled his mobile phone from his

to be on fire	brennen, in Flammen stehen
burning	brennend
to choke	ersticken, würgen

pocket. He called the emergency number. But just as he was about to speak, he saw a figure inside the house.

"There's someone in there!" he exclaimed.

"The witch!" Katie cried. "I told you. She's real!"

Michael threw the mobile to Alex, who immediately told the emergency services where they were. Then Michael climbed through the broken window into the **burning** house.

"Police!" he called out, but the figure had disappeared.

He ran through the room and into the hall. Spider's webs were on his face and in his hair. The fire seemed to come from the front room. He could feel how hot it was. He was **choking** on heavy smoke. He looked around, confused. Then he saw her: a woman was going up the stairs. He had no time. The fire was going to burn the old building down. He ran up the stairs. He could see quite well because of the orange glow from the fire. When he got to the top, he saw her standing very still, looking at him. For a moment, he thought that Katie was right. The woman was a witch.

Agnes Cott, he thought. She had long grey hair and dirty old clothes. She looked very old. Michael told her his name.

"I'm here to help you," he said.

She turned and ran down the corridor.

Michael followed her. He could see smoke from the fire coming up the stairs. He went into one of the bedrooms. Although it was darker in the room, he could see the old woman. She was trying to pick up some large, flat objects. When Michael got closer, he saw that the objects were paintings. On every one, he recognized Sylvia.

old people's home	Seniorenheim
to remember sth.	sich erinnern an
disease	Krankheit
care	Pflege, Betreuung

The old woman looked at Michael and started to cry.

"Please help me!" she said.

Two months later, after his evening shift, Michael left the station. He walked up the road. When he got to the **old people's home**, he stopped. Nigel Huxley was waiting for him. It was the same every Wednesday and Sunday. The two men went inside together.

Sometimes Sylvia couldn't **remember** their names. She couldn't remember pushing Lottie down the stairs, or laughing and knocking Michael out in the graveyard.

For weeks she'd been living in the old caretaker's cottage. She stole things to eat, as well as the paintings.

She couldn't be put in prison for her crimes because she had Alzheimer's **disease**. Instead, at the old people's home she had food, clothing and good **care**. She mainly remembered things that happened sixty years ago.

Michael knew she had been beautiful then, although he couldn't tell from looking at the

> Achten Sie immer auf den Unterschied zwischen **remind** und **remember**!
> **to remember sth.** sich erinnern an
> **to remind sb. of sth.** jmd. an etw. erinnern

old woman now. He and Nigel would listen to her stories about wonderful summer evenings, and her eyes would glow with happiness.

"Her eyes are the one thing that hasn't changed," Michael said to Nigel, looking at the photo of Sylvia in his wallet. "They're still beautiful."

Exercise 15: Questions about the text. Beantworten Sie die Fragen zum Text in ganzen Sätzen!

1. Who stole the Butterworth paintings and why?

   _____

   _____

2. Who was Agnes Cott?

   _____

3. What are the teenagers doing at the cemetery at night?

   _____

   _____

4. Why do the villagers think that the old caretaker's house is haunted?

   _____

5. Why is the gallery called the Oswald Gallery?

   _____

Catching a Big Fish

Sarah Trenker

A Wet Morning

Detective Henry Ramsey was angry, very angry. He didn't even wait for his young partner, Susan Mitchell, to close the car door before he started off down the road towards the harbour. It was raining. Susan groaned. The windows of Henry's old Mercedes always misted up when it was wet, and it was a long drive from Poole to Shelterwind Cove.

"Not a very nice day," Susan said as she quickly pulled on her safety belt. She tried to find space for her feet among the old newspapers and empty plastic cups on the floor. "But nice to get out of town for a change."

"Nice?" Henry shouted. "What do you mean by nice? This is the south of England, not the Côte d'Azur! What could possibly be nice about walking across a cold beach to look at a water-filled boat? And it's going to be a waste of time. We will probably find out that some idiot of a tourist sank the boat last spring."

Susan didn't answer. In his mid fifties, Henry was still a handsome man in a rough sort of way. But when he was in a bad mood, he looked a bit like a boxer before a fight. Susan de-

to groan	stöhnen
to mist up	(sich) beschlagen
cove	Bucht
safety belt	Sicherheitsgurt
among	zwischen
for a change	zur Abwechslung
waste of time	Zeitverschwendung
to sink	versenken; untergehen
handsome	gutaussehend
mood	Stimmung, Laune

cided it was better to leave him alone. She cleaned the passenger window with her sleeve and looked out at the boats as they drove along the beach road.

reason	Grund
case	*hier*: Fall; Koffer
demand	Forderung
narrow	eng

Anyway, she knew the real **reason** for Henry's anger. All the other detectives were on the big Churchill **case**. When they left the police station at 9 a.m., the others were listening to a tape of the kidnapper's **demands**. Detective Morgan, Henry's least favourite person at the office, did not help things. When he saw them walk by, he wished them a nice morning on the beach.

Neither of the detectives spoke again until they reached a little village, which marked about the halfway point between Poole and Shelterwind Cove. The **narrow** stone streets were almost empty. There were just a few old ladies under umbrellas, who were looking at postcards.

Exercise 1: Odd one out. Welches Wort ist das „schwarze Schaf"? Unterstreichen Sie das nicht in die Reihe passende Wort!

1. rain   wet   water   sand

2. town   school   village   city

3. irritation   rage   happiness   anger

4. detective   shop assistant   policeman   inspector

5. whisper   shout   sing   worry

6. car   lorry   bicycle   motorbike

"At least we won't **get caught up in** the usual **crowd** of tourists, now that the school holidays are over," Susan said. "It'll be easy to park …"

"Hmmph," came the **impatient** reply, as Henry **swerved** to miss a car which was coming out of one of the side roads. "Why didn't Chief Inspector Crawley ask us to help them find that millionaire James Churchill? That is far more important. Morgan is no good for jobs like that. He couldn't find a bowl of rice in a Chinese restaurant! It is a mystery to me how HE hopes to find the kidnapper without having to pay the **ransom**."

to get caught up in	in etw. verwickelt werden
crowd	Menschenmenge
impatient	ungeduldig
to swerve	ausweichen
ransom	Lösegeld
clue	Hinweis, Spur
envelope	Briefumschlag
to mumble	murmeln, nuscheln
to disappear	verschwinden
to waste	verschwenden
to sniff	schniefen

Again Henry swerved, this time to narrowly miss a duck that was sitting in the middle of the road.

"Anyway, why is he still at the station? He should be out looking for **clues**. Is he waiting for the kidnapper to send him another finger?"

Susan thought back to the **envelope** with Churchill's little finger and the tape which someone had put on the steps of the station the day before. "I hope not," she **mumbled**.

Henry took no notice of her. "I don't think anyone has even been down to the Royal Bath Hotel to look at Churchill's room – and he **disappeared** the day before yesterday! You don't need six people to listen to a tape recording! They are **wasting** time that could cost Churchill his life."

Detective Ramsey **sniffed** loudly. "One of the most exciting cases for a long time. We should be working on it, too. But no, they don't **trust** me since the accident. I get sent to look at stranded boats and see if I can find any dead bodies."

to trust	(ver)trauen
to nod	nicken
understand-able	verständlich
upset	aufgeregt, verärgert
horseshoe-shaped	hufeisenförmig

His partner **nodded**, but said nothing. What could she say? Since that horrible accident when the teen murderer had tried to get away...

It was **understandable** that Henry had been **upset**. Everyone at the office knew he liked his whisky, but for a while people thought he was an alcoholic. Even now, a year and a half later, their boss, Chief Inspector Crawley, still did not seem to want to give his old favourite much responsibility.

Exercise 2: Genitives. Übersetzen Sie mit s-Genitiv oder of-Genitiv!

1. die Mäntel der Detektive _____

2. Henrys Auto _____

3. die Farbe des Autos _____

4. das Schiff der Männer _____

5. der Fall des Entführers _____

6. die Schirme der alten Dame _____

7. die Länge des Briefes _____

In the empty car park at Shelterwind Cove, the two detectives pulled on their coats. Then they walked along the path past the small houses and down to the famous **horseshoe-shaped** cove.

Although there were about 15 small boats on the sand, it was easy to **recognize** the boat they were here to see. Next to the fishing boats, the shiny, red motorboat was as unusual as a mango in a box of apples.

"It doesn't look as though it was under water for very long," said Susan as they walked over to look at it.

"No, it doesn't," Henry agreed as he looked at a small hole in

to recognize	erkennen
hull	(Schiffs-)Rumpf
to report	melden, berichten; anzeigen
to get one's teeth into sth.	sich in etw. hineinknien
cabin	Kabine
obviously	offensichtlich
thief, thieves *pl*	Dieb
equipment	Ausrüstung
rope	Seil, Tau
drug runner	Drogenschmuggler

the **hull**. "But why didn't the owners **report** it? Or at least tell somebody about it?"

Something was not quite right here. Henry smiled for the first time that day. At last, something to **get his teeth into**. He felt better already. Why, it had even stopped raining!

Susan tied her long red hair back to stop it blowing into her face and waited for instructions.

"See if you can find anything on the beach near the boat," Henry said. "I'll have a look in the **cabin**."

Susan walked off, and Henry climbed onto the boat. Inside the cabin, there was very little water, which seemed to show the boat got to the beach soon after it hit the rock. **Obviously**, **thieves** had soon found the boat, because a lot of the boat's **equipment** was missing.

There was an expensive-looking **rope** in the corner, and Henry wondered why the visitors hadn't taken that. He examined it and realized that it was in a number of pieces. Something had been tied at the back of the cabin and then quickly cut free. Perhaps the people on the boat were **drug runners**, he thought. The boat was not really big enough to cross the Channel, but perhaps it had picked up a package from a sailboat near the coast and then got into difficulty during the bad weather.

Channel	Ärmelkanal
wrapper (of sweets)	(Bonbon-)Papier; Verpackung
kind	Art; Sorte
quay	Kai
to add	hinzufügen

The only other things left on the boat were a few sweet wrappers which were swimming in a pool of seawater at the bottom of the cabin. Henry recognized the wrappers immediately. Only one shop in the whole of Dorset[i] sold that kind of caramels. The sweet shop was one of the top places to visit on Poole Quay.

When Henry jumped off the boat, he found Susan with two fishermen – an older man with a boy of about sixteen.

"These two found the boat," she said.

"When was that?" asked Henry.

The older of the two fishermen answered. "Yesterday morning, when we came down to go fishing."

"And why didn't you phone the police until today?" Henry replied impatiently.

"We thought the owner would come back during the day," the fisherman said.

"And when he didn't, that's when Mrs Summer decided to tell the police," the second fisherman added. The way he said "Mrs Summer" made it clear that he was not at all pleased that she had phoned the police.

You still had enough time to take anything you liked from the boat, Henry thought, but he didn't say a word. Instead, he turned to Susan, "The boat has no name, so it will be quite difficult to find the owners, unless the owners report the loss themselves."

Die Grafschaft Dorset in Südengland ist bekannt für Seebäder mit schönen langen Sandstränden.

He turned back to the fishermen and added, "Do you know if there have been any **sudden** arrivals in the village? Especially people without cars?"

The older fisherman shook his head, but when he **was about to** say no, his teen **companion** interrupted.

sudden	plötzlich; unerwartet
to be about to do sth.	im Begriff sein, etw. zu tun
companion	Begleiter
common sense	gesunder Menschenverstand
to blush	rot werden, erröten

"What about that couple and their father who are staying at Mrs Cole's bed and breakfast? They arrived yesterday."

"They would hardly have come here in a boat," answered the first fisherman angrily. "You know the old man is very ill. Use some **common sense**."

The boy **blushed** and looked down.

"Well, thank you for your help anyway," Henry replied. "Susan, perhaps you could get the names and addresses of these two gentlemen? It is just a formality," he added when he saw the reaction of the fishermen. "We will probably not need to contact you again."

Exercise 3: Questions about the text. Beantworten Sie die folgenden Fragen zum Text!

1. Why do Susan and Henry drive to Shelterwind Cove?

   _____

2. Who do they see in the village they drive through?

   _____

3. Why did Henry start drinking too much?

   _____

Fishermen's Tales

News travelled fast in a small village like this, Henry thought. He was thus not surprised to see a **plump** woman of about his age in the door of the bed and breakfast hotel. She was waiting for them.

"You must be Mrs Cole," said Henry.

"Yes, and you must be the two detectives who have come to look at that stranded boat down on the beach."

"Detectives Ramsey and Mitchell," Henry smiled as he walked down the path **lined with** seashells.

In the garden next to the house was a small sailboat. In the wind, its **halyard whipped** noisily against the mast.

plump	mollig
lined with	gesäumt von
halyard	Leine zum Segelsetzen, Fall
to whip	schlagen, peitschen
identity card	(Dienst-)Ausweis
lounge	Wohnzimmer; Gesellschaftsraum
wallpaper	Tapete

"Could you show me your **identity card**, please?"

Susan pulled out her ID and showed it to Mrs Cole, who studied it carefully before giving it back.

"You'd better come in," Mrs Cole said. She turned and walked into a small **lounge**. Henry and Susan followed her.

Susan giggled when she saw the big yellow and orange flowers on the **wallpaper** and again when she saw the glass cats on the table.

"My goodness, this is the definition of an English bed and break-

to whisper   flüstern

fast house," she whispered as Mrs Cole walked across to the windows to pull back the curtains.

"How many guests have you got at the moment, Mrs Cole?"

"Just Mr and Mrs Hardy and Mrs Hardy's father, Mr Perry. They arrived from Salisbury early yesterday morning."

"Did they come by car?" asked Henry.

"I think they took a train to Bridport and then got into a taxi to come here. Mr Hardy had to almost carry Mr Perry upstairs. The poor man is very ill. I think they've taken him to the doctor this morning. I haven't heard anyone upstairs."

"Have you had other sudden visitors over the last couple of days?"

"No," Mrs Cole replied.

Exercise 4: Quantifiers. Unterstreichen Sie die richtige Mengenangabe!

1. There were not much / many boats on the beach.

2. How much / many diesel does the tank hold?

3. Harry didn't think it would be much / many fun on the beach in the rain.

4. How much / many people can you get in the boat?

5. Mrs Hardy asked Mrs Cole how much / many visitors she had.

6. Harry drank many / a lot of whisky after the accident.

7. James Churchill has many / a lot of money.

8. Much / A lot of people live in Poole.

98

"Are you the only bed and breakfast in the village?" Henry asked.

Susan giggled again.

"Mrs Penny also has a couple of rooms. She is four doors further down."

"Thank you for your help, Mrs Cole." Henry gave the woman his card.

to remember sth.	sich erinnern an
to snort	schnauben, prusten
There is more to it than meets the eye.	Da steckt mehr dahinter.
to glance up	aufblicken
direction	Richtung

"If you remember anything else that you think might be helpful, please let me know. We might come back and ask Mr and Mrs Hardy some questions later."

For the next hour, the two detectives walked from one house to the next and tried to find out if anyone had seen or heard anything. First, they visited the other bed and breakfast, but the two couples staying with Mrs Penny were both very old and therefore unlikely motorboat thieves. Afterwards, the two detectives separated and worked along opposite sides of the street. Nobody seemed to know anything, but everyone had a theory.

Susan laughed when she met Henry at the end of Sea View Road. "One more story about how easy it is to sink a boat here in winter, and I shall start to give everyone medals."

Henry snorted. "I still can't help thinking that there is more to this case than meets the eye."

He glanced up to see the younger of the two fishermen watching them from one of four small houses on the hill. When the boy saw the two detectives look in his direction, he turned away and quickly walked inside.

Susan looked at Henry and grinned. Henry grinned back. "Now doesn't he look like someone with something useful to say?"

"Oh yes," agreed Susan.

When the two detectives knocked on the door, they heard a lot of worried whispering before the young fisherman opened the door. He looked nervous.

Exercise 5: Simple present or present continuous?
Setzen Sie die Verben in die richtige Zeitform!

1. Henry and Susan **1. drive** _____ to work every day.
2. The fishermen **2. fish** _____ in the Cove at the moment.
3. Mrs Davies usually **3. rent** _____ rooms to tourists.
4. The people in Shelterwind village **4. eat** _____ a lot of fish.
5. Look out of the window and tell me if she **5. still smile** _____ ?
6. Mrs Cole **6. come** _____ on Thursdays.

"Hello, detectives," he said. "Have you had any luck? Were the tourists any help?"

"No, I'm afraid not," answered Henry. He checked the name Susan had written down in her notebook on the beach. "We hoped you might be able to give us a bit more information, Mr Bridges."

"Me?"

A woman came up behind the boy with a tea towel in her hand. She understood the situation at once. "So what's our Tom been doing this time?"

She was obviously the young man's mother.

I'm afraid (not)	leider (nicht)
tea towel	Geschirrtuch
at once	sofort

"I don't know that Tom has been doing anything wrong, Mrs Bridges. We just wanted to ask him a few questions. He and Mr...," Henry looked again at the notebook, "Lambert were very

to mutter	(vor sich hin) murmeln, brummeln
to get (straight) to the point	(gleich) auf den Punkt kommen
to believe	glauben

helpful earlier this morning. We are trying to find out who owns the boat stranded on the beach and what it is doing here."

"Should Tom go and get Dave Lambert? He lives next door."

"That will not be necessary, Mrs Bridges." Henry put on one of his most winning smiles. "We can always go and see Mr Lambert if necessary."

Susan nodded.

Exercise 6: Prepositions. Lesen Sie weiter und setzen Sie die richtigen Präpositionen ein!

in　into　to　of　on　to

Mrs Bridges nodded and asked them **1.** ____ follow her. They went **2.** ____ the kitchen and sat round the kitchen table **3.** ____ the corner.

"I don't know what you want me **4.** ____ tell you now," Tom **muttered**. "I told you everything I know this morning."

Henry **got straight to the point**. "Mr Bridges, I have reason to **believe** that someone may have taken some **5.** ____ the things that were **6.** ____ the boat."

Tom suddenly found his tea and the sugar bowl very interesting.

"That, of course, makes it very difficult for me to know where the boat came from and who it belonged to," Henry continued. "It makes me think that it might not be just theft we are looking for, but murder. An intelligent murderer would remove all the evidence from the boat, so that it would be difficult to trace the boat back to the owner."

"Are you saying you think my son is a murderer?" Mrs Bridges exclaimed angrily.

"Mrs Bridges, I think the fact that the boat has been picked clean does make the whole thing look suspiciously like murder."

Tom stopped stirring his tea. "I didn't have anything to do with any murder, honest!" Tom hesitated. "I might have taken a couple of things off the boat... The insurance will pay the owner – so, we... er... I decided to save some of the things that were still on it."

Mrs Bridges looked at Tom angrily. "What were you thinking, Tom? Go and get all of those things now."

"I can't. I don't have the stuff any longer."

"Where is it?" Mrs Bridges stood up.

Henry interrupted her before she could continue.

"Mrs Bridges, perhaps I should speak to your son alone for a while. It is very important that I find out exactly what he has done. Obviously, theft is not as serious as piracy!"

It was Mrs Bridges's turn to look nervous. "Piracy?" she muttered.

theft	Diebstahl
murder	Mord
evidence	Beweis(e)
to trace	aufspüren; (zurück)verfolgen
to exclaim	(aus)rufen
to pick clean	*hier*: ausplündern
suspiciously	verdächtig; misstrauisch
to stir (sth.)	(etw.) (um)rühren
to hesitate	zögern
insurance	Versicherung
serious	ernst
piracy	Piraterie
crime	Verbrechen

Exercise 7: Crime vocabulary. Setzen Sie die passenden Krimi-Wörter ein!

knife   body   evidence   kidnapper   rope
ransom

1. Henry found a piece of _____ on the boat.
2. They hid the _____ money at the bottom of the garden behind the big tree.
3. The police caught the _____ the next day.
4. They found Mrs Penny's _____ at the bottom of the pond.
5. The lawyer had enough _____ to win the case.
6. The wounds on the body showed that the murderer had used a _____ .

Susan saved the situation. "Mrs Bridges, perhaps you and I could talk together next door. I have some questions for you."

When the two were alone in the room, Henry quietly took out his notebook and put it on the table.

"Tom, I don't think you had anything to do with the missing crew, but taking things from a boat that doesn't belong to you is still a serious crime. What has happened to the things you took?" Henry asked.

"We took them to Weymouth. We met someone there that can sell the stuff."

"We?" Henry lifted an eyebrow.

Tom **shuffled his feet** nervously. "Dave Lambert and I occasionally sell the things we... find."

"And Dave Lambert is the man we saw with you this morning," said Henry.

"Yes, that's right."

Henry closed his notebook, the new page still clean, and put it in his pocket. "I think it is perhaps time to go and speak to your friend Mr Lambert."

The boy groaned. "He'll kill me..."

"He's not allowed to do that," replied Henry. "But don't worry, if he does kill you, I'll **arrest** him."

Henry smiled to himself when he saw Tom's face.

Although Henry was sure that Tom had had nothing to do with the disappearance of the crew from the boat, he was not as sure about Dave Lambert.

Exercise 8: True or false? Trifft die Aussage zu? Kreuzen Sie an!

1. Mrs Cole was a slim woman. ❑
2. Susan liked the decoration in the lounge of the bed and breakfast. ❑
3. There are two bed and breakfast hotels in Shelterwind Cove. ❑
4. Mrs Bridges was Tom Bridges's wife. ❑
5. Tom is a teenager. ❑
6. Henry doesn't think Tom has anything to do with the missing crew. ❑
7. Tom is a bit afraid of Dave Lambert. ❑

When Henry and Susan came to **question him**, the man was very aggressive and spoke in a deep, unpleasant voice that made him sound dangerous. One look from him had been enough to make Tom be quiet. "Like Tom said, we only took things from the boat after we found it on the beach," he **growled**. "I took the stuff into

to shuffle (one's feet)	mit den Füßen scharren, schlurfen
to arrest	verhaften
to question sb.	jmd. befragen
to growl	knurren, brummen
marina	Jachthafen
to scowl	mürrisch blicken
used to be	(mal) gewesen sein
common	häufig, (weit) verbreitet

Weymouth and found a man staying in the **marina** who bought it from me. That's why I can't tell you where to find him. I didn't ask his name, and he wanted to leave the next day."

Henry was sure that there was something that the fishermen were not telling them, but it seemed useless to question Dave Lambert any further.

When the two detectives left the house, Henry noticed a taxi parked in the porch. He looked at the fisherman.

"Did you find that, too?"

Lambert **scowled**. "No, that's mine. When fishing is bad, I earn a bit of extra money with the taxi. Do you want to see my licence?"

Detective Ramsey shook his head. "We need to find the owners of the boat. I think they may be drug runners. Lives may be in danger. Please tell me if you remember anything else about the man who bought the things from the boat."

The two detectives started to walk slowly back towards the car park. They were silent for a couple of minutes, then Susan muttered, "I'm not sure Dave Lambert told us all he knew."

"That makes two of us," answered Henry.

"Piracy **used to be** very **common** in these parts, didn't it?" asked Susan after a few minutes.

"Yes. In the old days, the people here used to **guide** the ships onto the rocks, kill the crew and then take all the **cargo**."

"Well, then I **suppose** we should be happy their great grandchil-

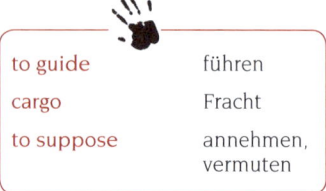

to guide	führen
cargo	Fracht
to suppose	annehmen, vermuten

dren are continuing their trade on a less murderous level," answered Susan.

"If only we could be sure," muttered Henry.

Susan nodded but said nothing.

When they were about to drive out of the car park, Tom ran towards them. Henry opened his window.

"You forgot your notebook, Detective Ramsey," the boy said loudly.

Henry was about to say his notebook was in his pocket when he saw the boy's worried face.

"Thank you, Tom," he replied equally loudly and took a piece of paper from Tom's hand.

"I didn't give you this," Tom whispered.

"And nobody here will ever know, but I shall remember," Henry replied quietly and drove off, leaving the boy standing alone in the car park.

"What is it?" Susan asked when Henry opened the piece of paper with one hand.

> Durch die Ergänzung **a piece of** werden unzählbare Nomen zählbar gemacht: *a piece of paper, a piece of information*

"If I'm right, it is the name of the man we need in Weymouth." Henry was right. It was.

Back in Town

On the way to Weymouth, Susan contacted Poole police station to let them know where they were and to find out if anyone had reported the boat missing in the meantime. Nobody had.

There was also nothing good to report on the Churchill case. Their colleagues had only found one new piece of information: At the time of the kidnapping, James Churchill seemed not to have been in the hotel at all. A man at the Royal Bath Hotel had seen him leave the hotel on foot at about 5 p.m. Otherwise, the only other news was that Churchill's manager in Poole, Russell Davies, was causing problems. He now phoned Richard Morton almost every hour to ask him to hurry up and hand over the ransom money. He knew from Churchill's son that the ransom money was already at the police station. He shouted angrily at Richard Morton every time he phoned.

"Probably because he is very worried about Churchill," said Susan when she told Henry about the phone call. "Churchill's son delivered the money almost immediately, so he can't understand why Morton hasn't organized a meeting with the kidnapper."

"Poor old Morton," Henry remarked, smiling. "I bet he wishes he could come to Weymouth with us now."

It was not hard to find the place on Tom's note. The "fish and bits" shop was the main centre of attention on the quay. It was clearly popular with both fisher-

| to bet | wetten |
| centre of attention | Zentrum der Aufmerksamkeit |

men and hobby sailors and was **bursting with** every kind of man and woman of the water. With so many people inside, it was difficult for the detectives to see who was **in charge**.

Eventually, however, a **bearded** man in a **Breton sweater** came over to help them.

"Can I help you?"

Henry nodded and held up his police **badge**.

The man's smile disappeared. "What's wrong?" he asked nervously.

"Are you the owner of this shop?" Henry quickly put away his ID and got out his notebook.

"Yes. My name is Bert Collins."

"Mr Collins, we have reason to

to burst with	überquellen von, platzen vor
in charge (of)	zuständig (für); leiten
bearded	bärtig, mit Bart
Breton sweater	Matrosenpullover
badge	Abzeichen
recently	kürzlich, jüngst
to grunt	brummeln; grunzen
to comment	(etw.) kommentieren

believe that you **recently** bought some second-hand boat parts which were on a boat stranded at Shelterwind Cove. Is that right?"

"Yes, that is right, from two local fishermen, who said they got the parts from an old boat that did not belong to anybody."

"That is not quite true," smiled Henry, who realized that the owner probably often bought boat parts from people who "found" them somewhere.

Customers were looking in their direction now. "I have the box out the back," said Bert and led the two detectives to a small room behind the shop. On the table was a cardboard box. "This is the stuff they brought me," he **grunted**.

"Is this all?" asked Henry. The box seemed very small. He looked into the box and waited for the man to **comment**, but he didn't. "I will have to take this box with me," he added.

"I paid good money for this equipment," said the manager angrily, "and have the receipt to prove it." "Mr Collins, do you know the difficulties you could get into if I reported the fact that you bought stolen goods to sell in your shop?"

"How was I supposed to know that the fishermen stole them?"

receipt	Quittung
to prove	beweisen
goods *pl*	Ware(n)
to assume	vermuten, annehmen
to swallow	schlucken
to remind sb. (of sth.)	jmd. (an etw.) erinnern
drug squad	Drogenfahndung

Susan snorted, and Henry laughed when he picked up the box. "I hope for you, Mr Collins, that everything is in this box, or there will be trouble... I would also advise you not to tell either of the two fishermen that we have picked up their box. Otherwise, I will have to assume that you often buy stolen goods..."

Bert Collins swallowed hard and shook his head. "I won't say a word," he promised.

On the way back to Poole police station, Henry asked Susan to phone Mrs Bridges. "Tell her to remind her son and Dave Lambert that they are now responsible for making sure that nothing else happens to that boat. If the owner appears, they should get his or her name and phone me immediately. Nobody may move the boat. Perhaps a team from the drug squad should go across to the village," he finished. "I'll talk to Inspector Crawley about it this afternoon."

The two detectives got back to Poole police station at lunchtime. Their colleagues seemed to be in almost exactly the same position they had been in at 9 a.m. However, the noisy activity was now a worried silence as the detectives waited for the telephone to ring.

"Hi, Richard. Have you had a nice morning in the office?" Henry asked.

Richard frowned and ignored the question.
Just at that moment, the telephone rang. Everyone jumped.
Richard Morton signalled to a colleague, and they both picked
up a phone receiver at the same time.
"Hello, Detective Morton speaking."

to frown	die Stirn runzeln
to jump	*hier:* erschrecken
receiver	Hörer
disguised	verstellt, getarnt
to transfer (money)	(Geld) über-weisen

A digitally disguised voice thun-
dered through the loudspeaker
of the telephone. "Detective Morton, how nice! Have you got the
little package ready for me yet? I
know you want to transfer the
money as soon as possible."
The sarcasm was obvious.

"We are worried about Mr Churchill," said Detective Morton, without answering the question. "We do not want to do the exchange on Brownsea Island. It will take us too long to get Mr Churchill to hospital."

"Oh, how **thoughtful** of you."

Everyone watched the computer that tried to find the caller, but as soon as it seemed to have found the location, the location moved again.

thoughtful	*hier*: aufmerksam; nachdenklich
to bang	knallen, poltern
threat	Drohung
strange	merkwürdig, seltsam
grimly	grimmig, streng
⚡ damn	verdammt, verflucht

"If you try to trace this call, you will not succeed," the man continued. Then there was the sound of a hand **banging** on a table. "I am getting a bit angry with you, Detective. You have had my instructions for over 24 hours. You have wasted time, and I don't like that. To show you just how much I don't like wasting time, I have sent you another package. That may convince you that I am serious in my **threat** to kill Churchill if you do not come up with the money this evening. Rather sad really, if you consider how well Churchill plays the piano – or should I say PLAYED...?"

The line went silent for a couple **ⓘ** of seconds except for a **strange** whipping noise in the background.

"Have you understood me, Morton?"

"Loud and clear," replied Detective Morton **grimly**.

The line went dead. Detective

Ähnlich wie im Deutschen bedeutet **couple** als Substantiv „Paar" (zwei Dinge/Menschen), als Pronomen (**a couple of**) aber „ein paar" (mehrere):

couple	Paar, Pärchen
a couple of	ein paar, einige

Morton looked over at his colleague at the computer, who shook his head.

"**Damn**! We're back to where we started. And it sounds like Churchill has lost another finger."

Henry was thoughtful for a moment. "Richard, that whipping noise. Do you know what it is?"

Richard looked up. "No, but it is there every time he rings, which would seem to confirm that he is not moving location."

"I know that sound from somewhere," said Henry. "I only wish I could remember where."

"That makes two of us," answered Richard. The two men smiled at each other for the first time in months.

A worried secretary came in. She had a package in her hands. "This one was outside on the wall, too," she said.

Exercise 10: Translation quiz. Übersetzen Sie die Begriffe, um das Rätsel zu lösen!

1. Hintergrund   _ _ _ ☐ _ _ _ _ _

2. Opfer   _ ☐ _ _ _

3. Mord   _ _ _ ☐ _ _

4. Lösegeld   _ _ ☐ _ _ _

5. Sarkasmus   _ _ _ _ ☐ _ _

6. Piraterie   ☐ _ _ _ _

7. Polizist   ☐ _ _ _ _ _ _

8. stehlen   _ _ ☐ _ _

9. Detektiv   ☐ _ _ _ _ _ _

Lösung: ☐ ☐ ☐ ☐ ☐ ☐ ☐ ☐

Henry left Richard and his team with the second parcel and was suddenly glad that he didn't have anything to do with the Churchill case. He and Susan went to his office and emptied the contents of the box onto his desk.

Susan picked up a **brass barometer**. "There is a small **nameplate** on this. Perhaps that might help us to find the owner."

"Can you read it?"

Susan held it under a lamp. "Well, it's pretty old. The brass has been cleaned so often that the nameplate is almost impossible to

to confirm	bestätigen
brass	Messing; aus Messing
barometer	Barometer, Luftdruckmesser
nameplate	Namensschild
competition	Wettbewerb
to wonder	sich fragen
waypoint	Wegpunkt

read. It seems it was a prize for a sailing **competition**. Yes, that's it. 'Winner of the 18th Brownsea Island Regatta, 1978.' There is no name."

"Well, it is a start at least," answered Henry. "Phone the Poole sailing clubs and try to find out which of them does a Brownsea Island Regatta. They should have lists of the winners."

While Susan was making the phone calls, Henry looked at the other items from the box. He picked up a GPS. He was no sailor, but he knew enough about GPS systems to **wonder** whether the person in charge of the boat had used **waypoints** to help him get from one place to the other. He turned the GPS on and played with it for a while until he found the waypoint programme.

"I've found it," he exclaimed.

Susan eyed him suspiciously. "What is it? Have you found a name?"

"No, not quite as good as that but almost. I have found the waypoints for the last trip. The boat left from the new marina on Poole quay. That marina is quite small, so we might find someone there who knows the boat."

Henry picked up the phone and rang directory enquiries. A woman gave him the telephone number of the marina and then connected him. A man answered the phone.

"Poole Quay Marina."

"Hello, this is Detective Ramsey from the Poole police station. I am phoning concerning a boat we found on the beach in Shelterwind Cove. I am hoping you might be able to help me find out who the owners are."

Exercise 11: Simple past. Formulieren Sie die Sätze im Simple Past!

1. The detective finds a clue on the beach.

   _____

2. It takes a long time to get from Poole Harbour to Shelterwind Cove.

   _____

3. Fishermen from Shelterwind Cove sell their fish at the market in Weymouth.

   _____

4. Dave Lambert goes fishing every day, but he also steals equipment from the boats he finds on the beach.

   _____

   _____

5. He puts the finger into an envelope and sends it to Poole police station.

   _____

"What kind of boat is it?"

"It is a bright red motorboat, one of those new French boats everybody has been talking about, Jeanmoreau, Jeaneau or something like that... It left your marina at about 2 p.m. [i] two days ago."

The man at the other end of the line thought for a moment, while Henry crossed his fingers.

"Yes, I know the one you mean," the man said suddenly. "That is the 'Carpe Diem'. It belongs to the Poole branch of Witan Holdings, but sometimes other people take it out. This time it was a man and his wife. They told me that they would be away for a couple of days, so I should not expect to see them before Sunday."

"Who told you they could take the boat out?"

"Russell Davies."

"Thank you very much!" Henry put down the phone.

Susan had also just put down the receiver. "Hurrah! I've got the name..." she shouted.

"Russell Davies by any chance?" asked Henry.

"Damn you," Susan laughed. "Hey, isn't Russell Davies the name of James Churchill's manager down here?"

"It is indeed!"

In the Net

Inspector Crawley's office at the police station always seemed like a palace compared with the small offices the rest of the team worked in. Henry had asked to speak to both him and Richard Morton about his latest discovery.

"So you mean to tell me that a boat that belongs to Witan Holdings disappeared on the same day as Churchill, and Russell Davies forgot to mention it?"

"Well, it could be that he hasn't even realized that it has gone missing if the man and woman said that they would be away until Sunday," Susan said.

"It could be," answered Inspector Crawley and looked at Richard Morton for his opinion.

"I agree with Susan," said Richard Morton. "Witan Holdings is an **enormous** company. It has come a long way since James Churchill opened the first branch in Dover. Now he has companies in all major **coastal** towns. The **headquarters** of Witan Holdings is in London – and Churchill's son will **take over** from his father next year."

enormous	riesig, enorm
coastal	Küsten…
headquarters	Zentrale, Hauptquartier
to take over	übernehmen, ablösen
to tie up loose ends	Unerledigtes erledigen

"The branch in Poole is very small. Why did James Churchill come down here?" asked Inspector Crawley.

"He is **tying up loose ends**. He wants to make sure his son does not have too many problems when he takes over the business.

He is closing some of the less profitable businesses. So, Poole might be on the list."

"Could he have been out on the motorboat?"

Richard Morton laughed. "No! He is almost seventy. The missing boat is probably just a coincidence."

coincidence	Zufall
to follow (sth.) up	(etw.) weiter-verfolgen
straight	direkt, gerade-wegs
to involve	*hier*: betreffen

"But I'm pretty sure that this is NOT just a coincidence! There is a connection between the two cases, and I would like to be able to follow it up," said Henry.

Inspector Crawley thought for a moment and then looked straight at Henry. "OK, Henry. I think Richard and his team have enough problems here at the moment. You and Susan should find out what happened to the two people on the boat and whether the coincidence involving Mr Davies and that boat in Shelterwind Cove is actually a connection."

Exercise 12: Unscramble the sentence. Bringen Sie die Wörter in die richtige Reihenfolge!

1. James Churchill why down come here did ?

_____

2. has receiver Susan just down the put

_____

3. got an Henry suddenly has idea

_____

Half an hour later, Henry and Susan drove into Witan Holdings in Poole. The car park at the building was full of birds – a sure sign that some really windy weather was on its way.

"What does Witan do?" Susan asked.

"Something in the **maritime** business," Henry answered. "Quite an old firm, but it was having money problems recently. James Churchill was thinking of selling the company. He was in Poole to talk to Russell Davies."

"Russell Davies must be worried!"

"Yes, I suppose so."

The woman at the **reception showed them in**. Russell Davies

maritime	See..., maritim
reception	Empfang
to show sb. in(to)	jmd. herein-führen
Chippendale (furniture)	teure Möbel-marke aus dem 18. Jahrhundert
to wave (one's hands)	winken
to get (straight) down to business	(gleich) zur Sache kommen
to suffer	leiden
sympathy	Mitgefühl
to match	passen zu; vergleichen

had an enormous office, which did not seem to have any money problems. On the floor, there was an expensive-looking carpet, old paintings of ships at sea hung on the walls, and Russell Davies was sitting behind a large **Chippendale** desk.

James Churchill's partner **waved** the detectives to two seats opposite his desk while he finished a phone call.

When he put the phone down, Russell Davies **got straight down to business**. "Hello, Detectives. I hope you are here to tell me that you will soon be able to give the kidnappers the money. I know the headquarters in London have already transferred the money. I think you have already wasted enough time. James has **suffered** enough."

Henry looked for a sign of **sympathy** to **match** the words but found none. Russell Davies was a hard businessman, he decided. He was a man who expected things to be done correctly and immediately.

"Detective Morton is waiting for the instructions from the kidnapper. Then we will do the exchange. Have you had any phone calls from the kidnapper?"

"No."

matter	Sache, Angelegenheit
concerned	besorgt
to hurt	*hier*: verletzen
to lend	(ver)leihen, borgen
to float	treiben, schwimmen
to appreciate sth.	etw. zu schätzen wissen

"We are here to ask about another matter. Has one of Witan's boats been reported missing?"

"Missing? No. What do you mean?" For a moment Russell Davies looked concerned.

"We have found one of your boats on the beach at Shelterwind Cove," Henry explained. "There was no sign of the crew, and we are worried that someone might have been hurt."

Russell Davies frowned. "I lent the boat to a couple of people from Norway. They phoned me yesterday to tell me that there had been a problem, but I was too busy to listen to what they had to say, I'm afraid."

"I need to talk to them," said Henry, examining Mr Davies closely. "They can't just walk off and leave a boat half floating in the water. It is very dangerous."

"You are right of course, Detective. But, as you know, I have had a lot to think about over the last few days."

"Yes, I do appreciate that. Could you give me the names of the two people who took the boat? I must talk to them."

Russell Davies hesitated. "I don't have their number here. I will get my secretary to give it to you later on today."

> Die Betonung mit dem **emphatic do** verstärkt eine Aussage und kann mit „tatsächlich" oder „sehr" übersetzt werden.
> **I do appreciate that.**
> Ich weiß das **sehr** zu schätzen.

"That would be good, Mr Davies. I shall wait for her call."
Henry stood up. "Thank you for your time. Come on, Susan."
Susan stood up and walked over to admire one of the paintings while Henry put on his coat.
"What lovely pictures you have in here," she smiled, her hand on the frame of one of the paintings.

Exercise 13: Unscramble. Lesen Sie weiter und bilden Sie sinnvolle Wörter aus dem Buchstabenchaos!

Outside, Henry turned to Susan, "So did you manage to bug the room while we were **1.** tikgnla _____?"
Susan **2.** slemid _____. "But of course, Henry. One on the phone and one on that big painting on the wall. What lovely pictures he has... What a joke! They're almost as boring as he is."
She giggled.
Henry grinned. "We'd better drive around the **3.** creron _____ - just in case he is watching us from his window."
Susan nodded in agreement.
Out of sight of the building, the **4.** dietvestec _____ parked next to a shop and turned on the receiver. For about five **5.** metisun _____, there was nothing suspicious about Russell Davies' behaviour. He told his secretary to organize some **6.** getimens _____ and send some letters.

However, as soon as she left the room, Russell Davies picked up the phone.

There was a pause as the telephone rang at the other end and somebody answered.

"I thought you said the boat sank," Russell Davies growled.

"Well, we thought it did." The woman at the end of the phone was nervous.

"Give me Paul!"

The receiver was passed from one hand to another.

to admire	bewundern
to manage to do sth.	es schaffen, etw. zu tun
to bug	verwanzen
just in case	nur für den Fall, dass …
sight	Sicht; Anblick
to run out of time	nicht (mehr) genug Zeit haben
⚡ to blow sth.	etw. vermasseln
morgue	Leichen-schauhaus
to call sth. off	etw. abblasen, absagen

"What do you want?" The man's voice was hard and unpleasant.

"Paul, you told me the boat sank."

"That was the plan. But it got changed. It wasn't my idea."

"Two detectives asked me about the boat. They even went to Shelterwind Cove to look at it – and they want YOUR names. We are running out of time. We are going to have to leave the country sooner than we thought."

"Yeah, I know." The man laughed.

"Where are you?"

"We're safe for the moment. That's all you need to know. My brother helped us find somewhere safe before the idiot almost blew everything."

The man's voice got louder. "Now, you just make sure we get the money. I only got two fingers from the morgue, so next time I really will have to cut off one of Churchill's fingers. The ransom must be delivered this evening, or we will have to call everything off. So phone the police station again and get things moving."

The line went dead.

A group of teens walked out of the shop. They met a woman outside whom they obviously knew and started talking to her. The sight seemed strange after listening to the kidnapper, Susan thought.

"If only we knew where they were," she muttered angrily.

"But we do," answered Henry suddenly. "Of course!" he shouted and hit the **steering wheel**. "But there isn't a minute to waste. Call up the station. Get them to send a couple of officers round to 'look after' Russell Davies. They should tell him that it is for his own safety. Whatever happens, the officers must not let him out of their sight, or allow him to make any more telephone calls. We don't want him to make any other bad decisions, do we?"

Susan was **confused**. "And where are we going?"

"Shelterwind Cove! But first I need to speak to Inspector Crawley and Detective Morton. We'll stop at the police station on our way." Thirty minutes later, the old Mercedes was back on the road to-

| steering wheel | Lenkrad |
| confused | verwirrt |

122

wards Shelterwind Cove. Henry felt nervous and happy at the same time. Now it all made sense: the whipping sound in the background when the kidnapper spoke to Richard Morton, the similar voices, the taxi driver. It seemed impossible that he had missed it before, but of course he had been look-

hiker	Wanderer/Wanderin
to wink	zwinkern
to set off	sich auf den Weg machen
slightly	etwas, ein bisschen
expression	(Gesichts-) Ausdruck
to harden	hart werden
to let sb. down	jmd. im Stich lassen

ing for a boat thief, not a kidnapper.

Henry parked in the main car park again. There were three other cars there which belonged to a large group of hikers. One of them looked up as Henry got out of the car smiling.

"Not the nicest of evenings for a hike," Henry said loudly.

"No, not really," answered one of the hikers equally loudly. "We only plan to walk to the hotel-pub at Shepherd's Lear tonight and then carry on tomorrow. Do you know the quickest way to get there, by any chance?"

"No, but Dave Lambert would know. He's a fisherman here and knows this area well. He lives in that house over there, the one with the taxi in the garage."

"Thank you." The hiker winked and set off to Dave Lambert's house with three of his companions.

Susan was feeling slightly sick while they walked down the beach path towards Mrs Cole's bed and breakfast. Henry looked at her. "Would you prefer to go and speak to Tom Bridges again?" he asked in a low voice.

"No." Susan's expression hardened. "I won't let you down. You don't have to worry."

Detective Ramsey nodded and smiled grimly. "Good. Everybody ready then," he muttered as if to himself.

He and Susan entered the gate of the bed and breakfast. It was still quite windy; the halyard of the small boat in the garden was banging against the house wall again and making its strange whipping sound.

Exercise 15: Comparatives. Bilden Sie die Steigerungsformen!

1. nice _____
2. confused _____
3. big _____
4. lovely _____
5. good _____
6. bad _____

Mrs Cole looked a bit impatient when she saw the detectives.
"Are you back again? I thought I'd answered all your questions this morning."
"You did, Mrs Cole, but as I said this morning, we would still like to speak to Mr and Mrs Hardy."
"Come in then." Mrs Cole took them back into the small lounge.
"Please tell Mr and Mrs Hardy that I need to speak to BOTH of them," said Henry.
Mrs Cole walked in a couple of minutes later with a man and a woman, both of whom looked about 35. They looked tense and had their hands in their pockets.
"Detective Ramsey, this is Mr and Mrs Hardy. I have told them that you just needed to ask them a couple of questions."

"Thank you, Mrs Cole, it was very kind of you to bring them in," answered Henry, smiling **firmly**. Mrs Cole understood the message. "Yes, right then, I'll be in the kitchen if you need me." With that she left the lounge and closed the door behind her.

tense	angespannt
firmly	fest, hart
to be (fast) asleep	(tief und fest) schlafen
briefly	kurz
opportunity	Gelegenheit, Möglichkeit
to burst in(to)	hereinstürzen

Henry held out a hand to Mr Hardy. "Good evening."

"How can we help you?" asked Mr Hardy, ignoring Henry's hand, his right hand firmly in his right-hand pocket. "We were just about to go out, now that my father-in-law **is asleep** at long last."

"You arrived here yesterday, Mrs Cole tells me. Is that correct?" Henry asked.

"Yes, we got a taxi from Bridport station and arrived yesterday morning," answered the woman. She was looking nervously at the man who stood next to her. He frowned at her.

"We would have been here a lot earlier if her father hadn't needed to stop the taxi every five minutes because he wasn't feeling well," her husband growled. "But anyway, why do you need to know?"

The man tried to smile, but he only managed a grimace.

Something broke in the kitchen and the noise made the man turn **briefly** towards the door.

Henry used the **opportunity**. He threw himself at the man and pushed him back onto the floor. Mr Hardy put his hand to his pocket but stopped as he saw the two guns pointed at him.

"Oh shit," he muttered angrily and put his hands up.

At the same moment, the door opened and two of the hikers **burst in**, both with guns in their hands.

"Everything under control, Detective Ramsey?"

"I think he has a gun in his pocket," answered Henry.

One of the hikers quickly removed a weapon from the man's pocket and put handcuffs on him.

handcuffs *pl*	Handschellen
special force	Spezialeinheit
to rush	eilen
staircase	Treppe
drugged	betäubt
shame	Schande; Scham
greedy	gierig

The woman started crying. "I always told you it was a bad idea," she said and put her hands up, too.

Susan walked over to her and removed a small gun from her pocket.

Everything suddenly seemed to be moving very fast, and the small house seemed even smaller. Mrs Cole was shouting angrily in the kitchen, while a large number of what looked like hikers, but were in fact special force policemen, rushed up the narrow staircase to the rooms upstairs.

"We found him," a man shouted down the stairs. "He is drugged but otherwise seems to be in good health."

"That's good for you, Mr Hardy, or should I call you Paul Lambert? That makes you Dave Lambert's brother, I believe?"

The handcuffed man scowled.

"Your brother gave you the perfect alibi by driving you here in his taxi after you'd left the boat, didn't he? Shame he got greedy and decided not to sink the boat. I suppose you picked up James Churchill from the beach. Did he go there to buy some of those sweets Russell Davies told you he loved? That must have been easy. What did you give Churchill to make him sleep?"

"Sleeping pills. He'll be all right in a few hours," Lambert replied angrily. "Anyway, how did you find us so quickly? There was nothing left on the boat to give you any clues."

Henry looked at Susan. "Should I tell him?"

Susan shook her head. "Oh no, let him work it out. After all, he's going to have enough time to think about it, isn't he?"

Final Test

Answers

Glossary

List of Exercises

Final Test

Exercise 1: True or false? Welche der folgenden Aussagen zur Geschichte „Learning by Killing" sind wahr? Markieren Sie mit richtig ✔ oder falsch – !

1. Eastcastle is a small town in the North of England. ❐
2. Colonel Lessons wants to retire to Brighton. ❐
3. Tracy Dean was born in Ireland. ❐
4. Jim Ryan is a Catholic from Dublin. ❐
5. Mrs Bradley is a cleaner at the school. ❐
6. Elke comes from Switzerland. ❐

Exercise 2: If or when? Setzen Sie in die Lücken das passende Wort ein!

1. Tracy enters the classroom to find out _____ everything is going smoothly.

2. Karl wants to check the words in his dictionary _____ he goes back in his hotel.

3. _____ all pupils learn their text by heart, the play will be a success.

4. There will be a future for Tracy and Jim _____ he loves her as much as she does.

5. _____ she realizes that he doesn't love her, she is very sad.

Exercise 3: Negative sentences. Bilden Sie verneinte Sätze!

1. Tracy thinks about the money in a brown envelope.

   _____

2. Inspector Watson is doing his interviews.

   _____

3. They had security cameras.

   _____

4. Joan gave Michael the keys to the gallery.

   _____

5. Henry and Susan have found the kidnapped man this morning.

   _____

Exercise 4: Verb forms. Setzen Sie die richtige Verbfom ein!

1. After the phone call was finished, Michael open _____

   _____ the car window.

2. He saw her rush _____ into the room, looking very frightened.

3. Two people hide _____ in some bushes underneath a tree.

4. Tomorrow, someone come _____ round and check for fingerprints.

Exercise 5: Word search. Finden Sie im Suchrätsel sieben Begriffe aus "The Butterworth Mystery"!

C	H	O	K	I	N	G	T	U	Z
Y	G	V	U	G	T	R	A	J	E
I	O	B	S	H	H	E	B	O	D
S	R	I	C	A	I	K	B	X	W
E	G	R	A	V	E	Y	A	R	D
M	E	X	R	I	F	L	Z	Q	B
I	O	H	Y	C	I	S	S	A	J
Z	U	P	A	I	N	T	I	N	G
O	S	F	L	T	W	A	F	M	E
P	Q	A	G	H	O	S	T	U	C

Exercise 6: Contracted forms. Bilden Sie die verneinte Kurzform!

1. I can   _____

2. I will   _____

3. I do   _____

4. you are   _____

5. we could   _____

6. it is   _____

7. he should   _____

Exercise 7: Verb forms. Wie heißt das Präsens der folgenden Verben?

1. felt	_____	**7.** went	_____
2. tried	_____	**8.** could	_____
3. began	_____	**9.** spoke	_____
4. sat	_____	**10.** saw	_____
5. fell	_____	**11.** froze	_____
6. put	_____	**12.** lent	_____

Exercise 8: Multiple choice. Welcher Satz enthält die richtige Übersetzung?

1. Was meinst du, Susan?
   a) ☐ What did you mean, Susan?
   b) ☐ What do you think, Susan?

2. Ich bin auf den Weg ins Polizeirevier.
   a) ☐ I am on my way to the police station.
   b) ☐ I am going in the police station.

3. Offensichtlich kannten sie die Fischer.
   a) ☐ They obviously knew about the fishermen.
   b) ☐ They obviously knew the fishermen.

4. Russel Davies fing an zu schreien.
   a) ☐ Russel Davies started to shout.
   b) ☐ Russel Davies started to cry.

Exercise 9: Vocabulary quiz. Lösen Sie das Kreuzworträtsel!

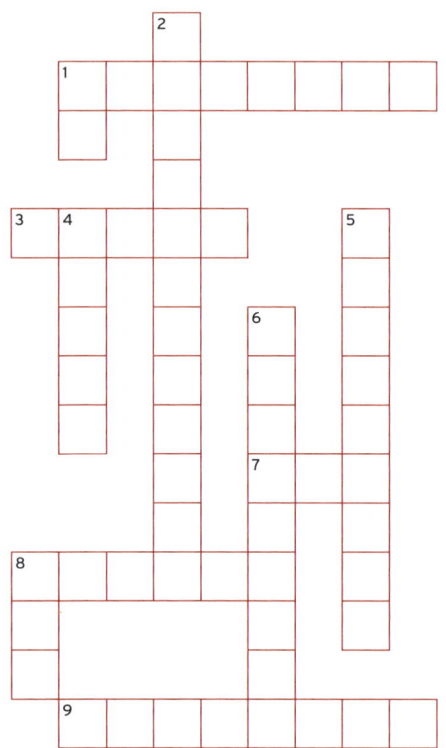

Down:

1. short form for police constable
2. clues left at the crime scene
4. a place where tourists stay at night
5. a policeman
6. a crime: a person threatens to give away secrets
8. to move very quickly

Across:

1. a piece of art
3. someone who steals
7. a tabby is a …
8. money paid for a kidnapped person
9. a crime: when thieves enter a house

Answers

Learning by Killing

Exercise 1: 1. laugh/cry 2. plump/slim 3. whisper/shout 4. cheap/expensive 5. late/early 6. short/tall 7. superb/terrible 8. heavy/light 9. fast/slow

Exercise 2: 1. ugly 2. car 3. garden 4. stay 5. clever 6. secretary 7. huge 8. seagull 9. sailor

Exercise 3: 1. smile 2. laugh 3. looks 4. come 5. means 6. know 7. think 8. can 9. produce 10. depends 11. have

Exercise 4: 1. magazine 2. desk 3. biro 4. briefcase 5. folder 6. chips 7. redhead 8. class

Exercise 5: 1. is 2. am talking 3. am trying 4. means 5. nods 6. says

Exercise 6: 1. You can put logs on a fire. 2. Karl picks up his biro. 3. Pierre speaks with a French accent. 4. People meet their friends in a pub. 5. She decides that Karl must die. 6. You are an innocent witness. 7. Jim is happy that the ice is broken.

Exercise 7: 1. false 2. false 3. false 4. true 5. false 6. false 7. true

Exercise 8: 1. by 2. about 3. for 4. at 5. out 6. off 7. off

Exercise 9: 1. cocky/impertinent 2. cut/commission

3. hip flask/bottle **4.** under false pretences/ illegally **5.** calm/relaxed **6.** grand/thousand **7.** vigorously/energetically

Exercise 10: **1.** think **2.** leaves **3.** runs **4.** hurries **5.** follows **6.** is lying **7.** is dying

Exercise 11: **1.** Sie sind bereit, ihre Aufgaben zu präsentieren. **2.** Die Studenten lachen und unterhalten sich. **3.** Sie freuen sich auf die Aufführung. **4.** Mahdi verschwindet hinter den/dem Vorhang. **5.** Ich fahre weg und dann schießt du. **6.** Karl putzt seine Brille. **7.** Einige Studenten fangen an zu weinen.

Exercise 12: **1.** was **2.** were **3.** understood **4.** left **5.** knew **6.** heard **7.** thought

Exercise 13: **1.** Ryan's class can give no useful information because they are upset. **2.** The toy gun cost £5.50. **3.** Olsen's seat was in the second row. **4.** Olsen heard three sounds. **5.** Tracy was at home on Friday. **6.** The cleaner's name is Mrs Bradley. **7.** Olsen lives in Denmark.

Exercise 14: **1.** Is Watson doing his interviews? **2.** Do they order another gin? **3.** Does he turn to the gun collection? **4.** Does his school pay local taxes? **5.** Is she cleaning the floor? **6.** Is the sun setting on Eastcastle?

The Butterworth Mystery

Exercise 1: **1.** Felder **2.** Dorf **3.** mitfühlend **4.** alt **5.** Häuschen **6.** geschehen **7.** Tor **8.** Gemälde

Exercise 2:	1. b 2. c 3. b
Exercise 3:	1. brought 2. had 3. walked 4. were 5. was 6. told 7. stood
Exercise 4:	1. e 2. g 3. f 4. c 5. b 6. d 7. a
Exercise 5:	1. Where 2. What 3. When 4. Which 5. Why 6. Who
Exercise 6:	1. After 2. about 3. at 4. to 5. in 6. with 7. for
Exercise 7:	1. e 2. c 3. f 4. h 5. a 6. g 7. i 8. d 9. b
Exercise 8:	1. quickly 2. close 3. serious 4. full 5. clear 6. alive
Exercise 9:	1. cook 2. torchlight 3. murderer 4. sell 5. box 6. museum 7. soldier 8. clue
Exercise 10:	1. mansion 2. torch 3. sculptor 4. mobile 5. cemetery 6. confident **Lösung:** stolen
Exercise 11:	1. went 2. wrote 3. heard 4. were living 5. to find 6. of 7. bring
Exercise 12:	1. false (He's 85.) 2. true 3. true 4. false (No, not without a search warrant.) 5. false (They lost contact much later.) 6. true
Exercise 13:	1. She 2. They 3. We 4. He 5. them 6. us 7. her 8. him 9. her 10. you
Exercise 14:	1. thieves 2. women 3. galleries 4. information 5. memories 6. noises 7. systems 8. witches
Exercise 15:	1. Sylvia Butterworth stole the paintings because she thinks they belong to her. 2. Agnes Cott was burned as a witch at Lancaster Castle in the 17th century.

3. They are bored and are partying at the cemetery. They are lighting candles and listening to music.

4. They think the house is haunted because sometimes strange noises can be heard and lights can be seen at the house.

5. It is named after John Oswald, who built the house the gallery is in.

Catching a Big Fish

Exercise 1:	**1.** sand **2.** school **3.** happiness **4.** shop assistant **5.** worry **6.** bicycle
Exercise 2:	**1.** the detectives' coats **2.** Henry's car **3.** the colour of the car **4.** the men's boat **5.** the case of the kidnapper **6.** the old ladies' umbrellas **7.** the length of the letter
Exercise 3:	**1.** They drive to Shelterwind Cove to look at a boat found on the beach. **2.** They see some women who are looking at postcards. **3.** There had been a horrible accident with a teen murderer.
Exercise 4:	**1.** many **2.** much **3.** much **4.** many **5.** many **6.** a lot of **7.** a lot of **8.** A lot of
Exercise 5:	**1.** drive **2.** are fishing **3.** rents **4.** eat **5.** is still smiling **6.** comes
Exercise 6:	**1.** to **2.** into **3.** in **4.** to **5.** of **6.** on
Exercise 7:	**1.** rope **2.** ransom **3.** kidnapper **4.** body **5.** evidence **6.** knife
Exercise 8:	**1.** false **2.** false **3.** true **4.** false **5.** false **6.** true **7.** true

Exercise 9:	1. dis- 2. un- 3. im- 4. un- 5. mis-
Exercise 10:	1. background 2. victim 3. murder 4. ransom 5. sarcasm 6. piracy 7. policeman 8. steal 9. detective **Lösung:** kidnapped
Exercise 11:	1. The detective found a clue on the beach. 2. It took a long time to get from Poole Harbour to Shelterwind Cove. 3. Fishermen from Shelterwind Cove sold their fish at the market in Weymouth. 4. Dave Lambert went fishing every day, but he also stole equipment from the boats he found on the beach. 5. He put the finger into an envelope and sent it to Poole police station.
Exercise 12:	1. Why did James Churchill come down here? 2. Susan has just put down the receiver. 3. Suddenly, Henry has got an idea.
Exercise 13:	1. talking 2. smiled 3. corner 4. detectives 5. minutes 6. meetings
Exercise 14:	1. suspicious 2. suspiciously 3. well 4. hard 5. easily
Exercise 15:	1. nicer 2. more confused 3. bigger 4. lovelier 5. better 6. worse

Final Test

Exercise 1:	1. false 2. false 3. false 4. false 5. true 6. true
Exercise 2:	1. if 2. when 3. If 4. if 5. When
Exercise 3:	1. Tracy does not/doesn't think about the money in a brown envelope. 2. Inspector Watson is not/isn't doing his interviews.

3. They did not/didn't have security cameras.
4. Joan did not/didn't give Michael the keys to the gallery. **5.** Henry and Susan have not/haven't found the kidnapped man this morning.

Exercise 4: **1.** opened **2.** rush **3.** were hiding **4.** will come

Exercise 5: **Across: 1.** CHOKING **2.** GRAVEYARD **3.** PAINTING **4.** GHOST
Down: 1. GORGEOUS **2.** SCARY **3.** THIEF

Exercise 6: **1.** I can't **2.** I won't **3.** I don't **4.** you aren't **5.** we couldn't **6.** it isn't **7.** he shouldn't

Exercise 7: **1.** feel **2.** try **3.** begin **4.** sit **5.** fall **6.** put **7.** go **8.** can **9.** speak **10.** see **11.** freeze **12.** lend

Exercise 8: **1.** b **2.** a **3.** b **4.** a

Exercise 9:

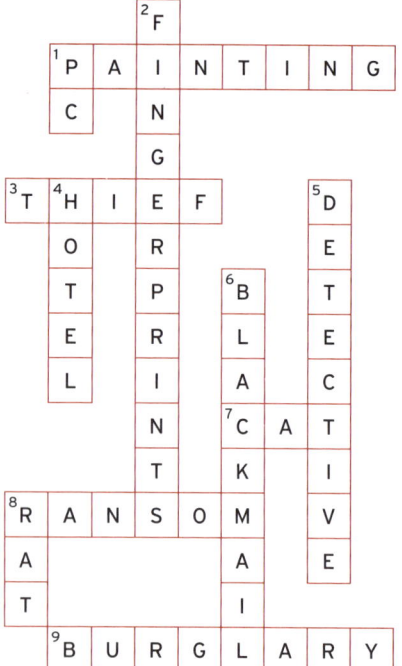

Glossary

↯ = umgangssprachlich
pl = Plural

accommodation	Unterkunft
accounts *pl*	Geschäftsbücher
actor/actress *m/f*	Schauspieler(in)
to add	hinzufügen
to adjust sth.	etw. zurechtrücken
to admire	bewundern
to afford	sich leisten
to alert sb.	jdn. alarmieren, warnen
allotment	Schrebergarten
allowance	*hier*: Beihilfe, Zulage
among	zwischen
apart from	außer
to apologize	(sich) entschuldigen
apparently	anscheinend
to appear	auftauchen, erscheinen
to appreciate sth.	etw. zu schätzen wissen
appreciation	Anerkennung
archive	Archiv
to arrest	verhaften
art restoration	Gemälderestaurierung
to assume	vermuten, annehmen
at once	sofort; gleichzeitig

attentive(ly)	aufmerksam
audience	Publikum
awkwardly	ungeschickt
badge	Abzeichen
badly	heftig, schwer
to bang	knallen, poltern
bangers and mash	Würstchen mit Kartoffelbrei
bargain	günstiges Angebot, Schnäppchen
barometer	Barometer, Luftdruckmesser
to be (fast) asleep	(tief und fest) schlafen
to be about to do sth.	im Begriff sein, etw. zu tun
to be involved in	beteiligt sein an
to be on fire	brennen, in Flammen stehen
to be performed	aufgeführt werden
to be sb.'s pride and joy	jds. ganzer Stolz sein
bearded	bärtig, mit Bart
bedsit	möbliertes Zimmer, Einzimmer-wohnung
to believe	glauben
to bet (bet, bet)	wetten
betrayal	Verrat
betrayed	betrogen; verraten
biro	Kugelschreiber
blackmail	Erpressung
blank	verständnislos, leer
⚡ to blow (blew, blown) sth.	etw. vermasseln
to blush	rot werden, erröten
to bow	(sich) verbeugen
branch	Niederlassung; Ast
brass	Messing; aus Messing
brave	mutig
to break the ice	das Eis brechen
to break the law	das Gesetz brechen
Breton sweater	Matrosenpullover

briefcase	Aktentasche
brief(ly)	kurz
bright	intelligent; hell; strahlend
to bug	verwanzen
bureaucracy	Bürokratie
burglary	Einbruch(-diebstahl)
to burgle sth.	einbrechen in
burning	brennend
to burst in(to)	hereinstürzen
to burst with	überquellen von, platzen vor
by (any) chance	zufällig, durch Zufall
by heart	auswendig
by the way	übrigens
cabin	Kabine
to call sth. off	etw. abblasen, absagen
canvas	Leinwand
care	Pflege, Betreuung
caretaker	Hausmeister
cargo	Fracht
case	Fall
to cast	*hier*: werfen
ceiling	(Zimmer-)Decke
cemetery	Friedhof
centre of attention	Zentrum der Aufmerksamkeit
Channel	Ärmelkanal
to chat	plaudern
cheerfully	fröhlich, heiter
Chippendale (furniture)	teure Möbelmarke aus dem 18. Jahrhundert
to choke	ersticken; würgen
to chuckle	kichern, in sich hineinlachen
church hall	Gemeindesaal
to clap	klatschen
clue	Hinweis, Spur
coastal	Küsten...

⚡ cocky	großspurig, frech
coincidence	Zufall
to comment	(etw.) kommentieren
common	häufig, (weit) verbreitet
common sense	gesunder Menschenverstand
community	Gemeinschaft
companion	Begleiter(in)
competition	Wettbewerb
complexion	Teint
concerned	besorgt
confidence	(Selbst-)Vertrauen, Zuversicht
confident	selbstsicher; zuversichtlich
to confirm	bestätigen
confused	verwirrt
confusing	verwirrend
⚡ conman	Schwindler
constable	Wachtmeister, Polizist(in)
contract	Vertrag
convincing	überzeugend
corpse	Leiche
cove	Bucht
crime	Verbrechen
crime scene	Tatort
Crimestoppers number	Telefonnummer für sachdienliche Hinweise
to cross one's fingers	die Daumen drücken
crowd	Menschenmenge
curtain	Vorhang
cut	*hier*: Anteil, Provision; Schnitt
⚡ damn	verdammt, verflucht
dare	Mutprobe
database	Datenbank
to deal (dealt, dealt) with	sich beschäftigen mit, zu tun haben mit
dedicated	engagiert

demand	Forderung
to depend on	abhängen von
detective work	Ermittlungsarbeit
to dial	wählen
direction	Richtung
directory enquiries	Telefonauskunft
to disappear	verschwinden
to disappoint sb.	jdn. enttäuschen
disease	Krankheit
disguised	verstellt, getarnt
Dorset	Grafschaft in Südengland
down	*hier*: offen, lose
dress rehearsal	Generalprobe
drive(way)	Auffahrt zu einem Haus
drug runner	Drogenschmuggler(in)
drug squad	Drogenfahndung
drugged	betäubt
eavesdropper	Lauscher(in)
edge	Rand, Ecke
elderly	älter
embarrassed	verlegen
emergency	Notfall
to emphasize	betonen, hervorheben
encouraging(ly)	ermutigend
enormous	riesig, enorm
to envelop	einhüllen
envelope	Briefumschlag
equipment	Ausrüstung
evidence	Beweis(e)
to exchange	wechseln, austauschen
to exclaim	ausrufen
exhibition	Ausstellung
to exist	bestehen, existieren
to explore	erkunden
expression	(Gesichts-)Ausdruck

fairly	ziemlich
familiar (with)	vertraut (mit), sich auskennen (mit)
fault	Fehler
fee	*hier*: Schulgeld; Gebühr
to feel at ease	sich wohl fühlen
fellow	Kerl, Bursche
figure	Gestalt; Figur
file	Akte
filing cabinet	Aktenschrank
fingerprint	Fingerabdruck
fire precautions *pl*	Brandschutzmaßnahmen
fireplace	(offener) Kamin
fireproof	brandsicher, feuerfest
firm(ly)	fest, hart
to float	treiben, schwimmen
to flow	fließen
to follow (sth.) up	(etw.) weiterverfolgen
for a change	zur Abwechslung
forensics	Kriminaltechnik
frantic	völlig verzweifelt
fright	Schreck
to frighten sb.	jdn. erschrecken
to frown	die Stirn runzeln
to gather	(ein)sammeln; (sich) versammeln
to get caught up in	in etw. verwickelt werden
to get one's teeth into sth.	sich in etw. hineinknien
to get sth. off one's chest	sich etw. von der Seele reden
to get (straight) down to business	(gleich) zur Sache kommen
to get (straight) to the point	(gleich) auf den Punkt kommen
ghost	Gespenst
to giggle	kichern

to glance up	aufblicken
glasses *pl*	Brille; Gläser
glow	Leuchten
to glow	leuchten
to go (went, gone) off	*hier*: losgehen
goods *pl*	Ware(n)
gorgeous	herrlich, wunderschön
⚡ grand	tausend Pfund
grave	Grab
graveyard	Friedhof
greedy	gierig
to greet sb.	jdn. grüßen
grimly	grimmig, streng
to groan	stöhnen
to growl	knurren, brummen
to grunt	brummeln; grunzen
guardian	Wächter(in)
to guide	führen
gulp	(großer) Schluck
hall	Flur; Saal
halyard	Leine zum Segelsetzen, Fall
to hand in one's notice	kündigen
handcuffs *pl*	Handschellen
handsome	gutaussehend
to hang sb.	jdn. erhängen
to harden	hart werden
to haunt	spuken (in)
headquarters	Zentrale, Hauptquartier
headstone	Grabstein
to hesitate	zögern
to hide (hid, hidden)	(sich) verstecken
hiker	Wanderer(in)
hip flask	Flachmann
to hire	einstellen, anheuern
honeymoon	Flitterwochen

horseshoe-shaped	hufeisenförmig
housekeeper	Haushälterin
hull	(Schiffs-)Rumpf
to hum	summen
to hurt (hurt, hurt)	verletzen; schmerzen
I'm afraid (not)	leider (nicht)
identity card	(Dienst-)Ausweis
imagination	Fantasie; Vorstellung
impatient	ungeduldig
impertinence	Frechheit, Dreistigkeit
impostor	Betrüger(in)
impressed	beeindruckt
in charge (of)	verantwortlich, zuständig (für); leiten
incident	Zwischenfall, Ereignis
innocent	unschuldig; ahnungslos
insulting	beleidigend
insurance	Versicherung
to interview	befragen, verhören
investigation	Ermittlung, Untersuchung
to involve	*hier*: betreffen
involved	verwickelt, involviert
It's none of your business!	Das geht dich nichts an!
jealous	eifersüchtig
jumble sale	Flohmarkt, Basar
to jump	*hier*: erschrecken
just in case	nur für den Fall, dass …
kind	Art, Sorte
to knock over	umwerfen, umstoßen
Lancashire	engl. Grafschaft, benannt nach der Stadt Lancaster
landlord	Vermieter; Gastwirt
landscape	Landschaft
to lend (lent, lent)	(ver)leihen, borgen

to let (let, let) sb. down	jdn. im Stich lassen
⚡ Let's call it a day.	Machen wir Schluss (für heute).
lined with	gesäumt von
to look forward to	sich freuen auf
to loosen one's collar	den Kragen lockern
lounge	Wohnzimmer; Gesellschaftsraum
magic spell	Zauberspruch
to make a mental note of sth.	sich etw. merken
male	männlich
to manage to do sth.	es schaffen, etw. zu tun
mansion	Villa, Herrenhaus
marina	Jachthafen
maritime	See…, maritim
marvellous	wunderbar, fantastisch
match	*hier*: Treffer
to match (with)	(zusammen)passen; vergleichen (mit)
matter	Sache, Angelegenheit
meanwhile	währenddessen
mellowed brickwork	alter Ziegelsteinbau
memory	Erinnerung
to mind sth.	etw. dagegen haben
mist	Nebel
to mist up	(sich) beschlagen
mobile	Handy
mock	*hier*: gespielt; falsch
modest(ly)	bescheiden
⚡ money for old rope	leicht verdientes Geld
mood	Stimmung, Laune
⚡ moonlighting	Schwarzarbeit
to mop	wischen
morgue	Leichenschauhaus
to mumble	murmeln, nuscheln
murder	Mord

to mutter	(vor sich hin)murmeln, brummeln
nameplate	Namensschild
narrow	eng
nearby	in der Nähe
to nod	nicken
note	Notiz, Zettel
obsessed (with)	besessen (von)
obvious(ly)	offensichtlich
to offend	kränken, beleidigen
to offer	(an)bieten
old people's home	Seniorenheim
old-fashioned	altmodisch
opportunity	Gelegenheit, Möglichkeit
out of the blue	unerwartet, aus heiterem Himmel
passionate(ly)	leidenschaftlich
patroness	Mäzenin
to pay sb. a visit	jdm. einen Besuch abstatten
PC (Police Constable)	Polizist(in)
pebble	Kieselstein
⚡ pep talk	aufmunternde Worte
to pick clean	*hier*: ausplündern
piracy	Piraterie
plump	pummelig, mollig
to point (to)	zeigen (auf)
praise	Lob
prison	Gefängnis
promotion	Beförderung
property	*hier*: Immobilien
props *pl*	Requisiten
proud(ly)	stolz
to prove (proved, proven)	beweisen
Punch and Judy show	Kasperletheater
to purr	schnurren
quay	Kai

to question sb.	jdn. befragen
ransom	Lösegeld
rather	eher, ziemlich
reason	Grund
receipt	Quittung
receiver	Hörer
recent(ly)	kürzlich, jüngst
reception	Empfang
recipe	Kochrezept
to recognize	erkennen
relieved	erleichtert
to remember sth.	sich erinnern an
to remind sb. (of sth.)	jdn. (an etw.) erinnern
to report	melden, berichten; anzeigen
to rest in peace	in Frieden ruhen
right away	sofort
⚡ to roar off	davondonnern
robbery	Raubüberfall
rope	Seil, Tau
to run (ran, run)	*hier*: leiten
to run out of time	nicht (mehr) genug Zeit haben
to rush	eilen, sich beeilen
sack race	Sackhüpfen
safcty belt	Sicherheitsgurt
scapegoat	Sündenbock
to scowl	mürrisch blicken
to scramble	stürzen, hasten
to scream	schreien, kreischen
sculptor	Bildhauer(in)
sea shanty	Seemannslied
search warrant	Durchsuchungsbefehl
security	Sicherheit
security camera	Überwachungskamera
⚡ to send daggers	tödliche Blicke zuwerfen
serious(ly)	ernst

to set (set, set)	*hier*: untergehen
to set (set, set) off	sich auf den Weg machen
setting	Schauplatz
to settle back	sich zurücklehnen
shadow	Schatten
shame	Schande; Scham
shepherd's pie	Auflauf aus Hackfleisch und Kartoffelbrei
shift	Schicht(dienst)
to shiver	zittern
to show sb. in(to)	jdn. hereinführen
to shrug	die Achseln zucken
to shuffle (one's feet)	mit den Füßen scharren, schlurfen
shy(ly)	schüchtern
to sigh	seufzen
sight	Sicht; Anblick
to silence	zum Schweigen bringen
to sink (sank, sunk)	versenken; untergehen
to sip	nippen
siren	Sirene
to slam	zuschlagen, zuknallen
slightly	etwas, ein bisschen
to smash	zerschlagen, zerschmettern
to smirk	süffisant lächeln
smoothly	problemlos, reibungslos
to sniff	schniefen
to snort	schnauben, prusten
soldier	Soldat(in)
solution	Lösung
to solve	lösen
to sort sth. out	etw. regeln
to sparkle	funkeln
special force	Spezialeinheit
speck	Körnchen; Pünktchen
spider's web	Spinnennetz

to splutter	hervorstoßen, stammeln
spray paint	Sprühfarbe
staff	Kollegium; Personal
staircase	Treppe
to stare	starren
stay	Aufenthalt
to steal (stole, stolen)	stehlen
steering wheel	Lenkrad
still-life	Stillleben
to stir (sth.)	(etw.) (um)rühren
to stop by	vorbeischauen
straight	direkt, geradewegs
strange	merkwürdig, seltsam
stranger	Fremde(r)
stunned	benommen; fassungslos
success	Erfolg
successful(ly)	erfolgreich
sudden(ly)	plötzlich; unerwartet
to suffer	leiden
to suppose	annehmen, vermuten
to suspect	verdächtigen
suspicious(ly)	misstrauisch; verdächtig
to swallow	schlucken
to sweat	schwitzen
to swerve	ausweichen
to switch on	anschalten (Motor) anlassen
sympathy	Mitgefühl
tabby	getigerte Katze
to take (took, taken) over	übernehmen, ablösen
tax-free	steuerfrei
tea towel	Geschirrtuch
temptation	Versuchung
tense	angespannt
terror alert	Terroralarm
Thank goodness!	Gott sei Dank!

theft	Diebstahl
There is more to it than meets the eye.	Da steckt mehr dahinter.
thief, thieves *pl*	Dieb(in)
to think long and hard	es sich reiflich überlegen
thoughtful(ly)	*hier*: aufmerksam; nachdenklich
threat	Drohung
thrilled	begeistert, hingerissen
thud	dumpfes Geräusch
to tick off	abhaken
⚡ to tickle sb.'s fancy	jdn. reizen
to tie up loose ends	Unerledigtes erledigen
ties *pl*	Bindungen
⚡ tiff	Geplänkel, kleiner Streit
toad-in-the-hole	in Teig gebackene Würstchen
torch	Taschenlampe
to trace	aufspüren; (zurück)verfolgen
trail	Spur
tranquillity	Stille
to transfer (money)	(Geld) überweisen
to trust	(ver)trauen
unconscious	bewusstlos
under false pretences	unter Vorspiegelung falscher Tatsachen
understandable	verständlich
to unpack	auspacken
unsolved	ungelöst
upset	aufgeregt, verärgert
to upset sb.	jdn. ärgern
used to be	(mal) gewesen sein
vigorously	energisch, kräftig
violent	gewalttätig, brutal
volume	*hier*: Band, Buch
wallet	Geldbeutel
wallpaper	Tapete

to waste	verschwenden
waste of time	Zeitverschwendung
to wave (one's hands)	winken
wavy	gewellt
waypoint	Wegpunkt
to whip	schlagen, peitschen
to whisper	flüstern
to whistle	pfeifen
white as a sheet	kreidebleich
wig	Perücke
to wink	zwinkern
witch	Hexe
witness	Zeuge, Zeugin
witty	geistreich, witzig
to wonder	sich fragen
wrapper (of sweets)	(Bonbon-)Papier; Verpackung
wrinkle	(Gesichts-)Falte
to yell	(laut) schreien

List of Exercises

Lernkrimi Lektüren Englisch

Lernkrimi Lektüren Englisch

Bloody Diamonds
Classic
ISBN 978-3-8174-9494-1

Nobody Dies Twice
Classic
ISBN 978-3-8174-9495-8

In Terror
Lernthriller
ISBN 978-3-8174-8857-5

A Scottish Murder Mystery
Classic
ISBN 978-3-8174-8379-2

Keep Calm and Carry On Killing
Classic
ISBN 978-3-8174-1644-8

Lernkrimi Comic Englisch

Chasing Bloody Mary
ISBN 978-3-8174-1655-4

Lernkrimi Sprachkurs Englisch

Lernkrimi Sprachkurs
ISBN 978-3-8174-7844-5

Lernkrimi Hörbücher Englisch

 A1

Black Wedding
ISBN 978-3-8174-1817-6

Dangerous Deals
ISBN 978-3-8174-9988-5

 A2

A Shot in the Night
ISBN 978-3-8174-8202-3

The Butterworth Mystery
ISBN 978-3-8174-8203-0

Death Wish
ISBN 978-3-8174-8204-7

Strangled
ISBN 978-3-8174-1876-3

 B1

Bloody Revenge
ISBN 978-3-8174-8860-5

B2

Bloody Legacy
ISBN 978-3-8174-7676-3

Crime & Company
ISBN 978-3-8174-8976-3

Murder at the Office
ISBN 978-3-8174-7747-0

Lernkrimi Rätselblöcke Englisch

 A1

Murderous Games
ISBN 978-3-8174-9500-9

 A2

The Art of Crime
ISBN 978-3-8174-9155-1

 B1

A Deadly Puzzle
ISBN 978-3-8174-8832-2

Englisch lernen für geübte Anfänger

ISBN 978-3-8174-8203-0

Spannendes Hörerlebnis

A2

Der in diesem Band enthaltene Kurzkrimi **The Butterworth Mystery** jetzt auch als Hörbuch:
Audio-CD mit Begleitbuch
Gelesen von Muttersprachlern
Ca. 60 Minuten packender Krimispaß

Weitere Lernkrimi Hörbücher für das Sprachniveau A2:
Death Wish
(ISBN 978-3-8174-8204-7)
Strangled
(ISBN 978-3-8174-1876-3)

ISBN 978-3-8174-1764-3

Übung macht den Meister

A2/B1

Das Übungsbuch ist ideal für geübte Anfänger und Wiedereinsteiger, die ihre Englischkenntnisse auffrischen und vertiefen möchten.

Rund 200 thematisch sortierte Übungen zu Wortschatz und Grammatik

Inklusive Infokästen, Lösungen und Glossar im Anhang

Extra: Krimilektüre für geübte Anfänger – so wird das Sprachtraining noch spannender!